"Of course, we've come to expect celest
cally elevated thoughts from Kushner, autnor of *A Bright Room Called Day, Slavs!* and the Pulitzer Prize– and Tony Award–winning opus *Angels in America*. We've also come to expect plays that aren't neat and tidy, that force you to engage rather than passively absorb and don't let you race home in time to catch the eleven o'clock news . . . Few, if any, modern English-language playwrights of ideas can match Kushner's intellectual sweep, his subtle but razor-edged sense of humor and his gift for peeling back layers of character until we finally see the naked human within. Even fewer can equal his fiery moral passion or sheer gutsiness. With *Homebody/Kabul* Kushner has dared to walk through a contemporary minefield, a dramatic terra incognita, without the benefit of a Baedeker to guide him, and emerged intact on the other side with a powerful story to tell."

—REED JOHNSON, *LOS ANGELES TIMES*

"Searing . . . Kushner's use of language and ideas continues to make us think about the deeper questions . . . a masterful conglomerate of words, ideas and history."

—MARY HOULIHAN, *CHICAGO SUN-TIMES*

"Brilliant . . . this is a play for those who are interested in the root causes that preceded September 11, for those who can see through the fog of patriotism to the finer distinctions, who are finally ready to ask how on earth do we get out of this godforsaken place, who can bear to contemplate the thought that we have participated to some extent in our own tragedy."

—JAMES RESTON, JR., *AMERICAN THEATRE*

"Kushner, a writer who is always on high alert to humanity as well as history, has, in the Homebody, created a character—an 'impassioned, fluttery, doomed' character—who is timeless as well as timely."

—NANCY FRANKLIN, *NEW YORKER*

"*Homebody/Kabul* is a welcome payoff for all who've been waiting a decade for a worthy follow-up to Kushner's landmark *Angels in America*. Kushner's plunge into the murky whirlpools of Afghan history, culture and politics is astonishing in its intellectual scope. It is also fierce in its dramatic engagement with complex realities and deeply humane. Kushner has led and provoked our minds as richly as he's engaged our sympathies."

—ROBERT HURWITT, *SAN FRANCISCO CHRONICLE*

"An extraordinary play . . . a deeply felt expansively ruminative drama."

—PAUL TAYLOR, *INDEPENDENT* **(LONDON)**

"At a couple of points in her awe-inspiring hour-long monologue that opens *Homebody/Kabul*, the title character insists, 'I love, love, love the world.' In both its simplicity and complexity, the sentence shows why Kushner is America's most interesting and important playwright. He writes in big, bold, often beautiful declarative sentences where many of his colleagues write between the lines, where what is said in parentheses, or unsaid in ellipses, supposedly speak volumes. His characters step out to remake the world, or at least their own broken selves, where others sit miserably in an interior chamber room, both psychologically and geographically. *Homebody/Kabul* is as fine a piece of American theater as anything since his last epic, *Angels in America*."

—ED SIEGAL, *BOSTON GLOBE*

"Dazzlingly written, insightful and timely. The playwright's generous viewpoint is liberal and progressive. His language is rich, his canvas is vast and his storytelling dynamic."

—MICHAEL SOMMERS, *NEWARK STAR-LEDGER*

"*Homebody/Kabul* is a rich and intelligent piece." **—PETER BROOK**

"This is a haunting and beautiful play in spite of its author's best efforts to ruin it."

—JOHN PODHORETZ, *WEEKLY STANDARD*

HOMEBODY/KABUL

HOMEBODY/KABUL

TONY KUSHNER

REVISED VERSION

THEATRE COMMUNICATIONS GROUP
NEW YORK
2004

Homebody/Kabul is published by Theatre Communications Group, Inc., 520 Eighth Ave., New York, NY 10018-4156.

This publication is made possible in part with public funds from the New York State Council on the Arts, a State Agency.

TCG books are exclusively distributed to the book trade by Consortium Book Sales and Distribution, 1045 Westgate Dr., St. Paul, MN 55114.

LIBRARY OF CONGRESS CATALOGING-IN-PUBLICATION DATA
Kushner, Tony.
Homebody/Kabul / by Tony Kushner.
p. cm.
"Revised version"—T.p. verso.
ISBN 1-55936-239-1 (pbk. : alk. paper)
1. Kåbol (Afghanistan)—Drama. 2. British—Afghanistan—Drama.
3. Missing persons—Drama. I. Title.

PS3561.U778 H66   2004
812'.54—dc22   2004024028

Book design and composition by Lisa Govan
Cover design by Susan Mitchell
Cover art "Mummy," mixed media, 2001 by Lesley Kushner
Cover photograph by Christian Carone

First Edition, May 2002
Revised Version, December 2004

For my dear friend Kika Markham,
who asked me for a monologue,
and in memory of my mother
Sylvia Deutscher Kushner

CONTENTS

A FOREWORD

I saw the original production of *Homebody/Kabul* at New York Theatre Workshop in December of 2001. It was an uncanny experience. We were all of us—and New Yorkers especially—still reeling from the events of September the 11th, and here was this play, obviously written long before September of 2001, set in Afghanistan, expressing precisely the politics and conflicts that had suddenly burst onto the world stage. So much of the play's original reception was concentrated, quite naturally, on this strange confluence of events. One wondered, perhaps, if the play could survive its moment: would the sensationalism of its public birth at this critical historical moment overwhelm an experience of the play . . . as a PLAY? Could *Homebody/Kabul* receive a reading that concentrated on its intrinsic force as a human drama (instead of as a record of extrinsic world events)? (Did it *want* to? *Should* it?)

The fact that those questions arise reveals something central about the vision of the playwright, Tony Kushner. Tony is on record as describing the birth of the play as originating in his relationship with his mother and the experience of her death. He began the play as a monologue, written specifically for an actress-friend, delivered by the character of the Homebody—a woman pinioned between irony and sorrow in her recognition of her deficiencies as a wife and a mother. Afghanistan enters into this domestic imagining as the site of escape: a country whose history is recounted by the Homebody from gleanings gained from an antiquated tour book. The Homebody is, herself, a tourist to her life—a woman guided in her intimate relationships by the conviction that "all touch corrupts." Afghanistan represents the possibility of her own disappearance—a loss of the domestic containment of marriage and motherhood, an escape from the language that both defines and isolates her. We watch her don her coat and walk away from the parlor of her English home and into the world of Afghanistan. We follow her into the streets of Kabul and in the same gesture, she disappears and we are left in the company of her husband and daughter who, like us, have arrived in Afghanistan in search of the Homebody. Inevitably, all of Afghanistan opens into view: locating this Western woman, a tourist in Afghanistan gone missing, brings us into contact with all of the currents shaping Afghani society: the personal becomes the political.

It is the ease with which this transposition is effected—from the personal to the political, from the local to the global—that constitutes Tony's work as a playwright. That he began the play out of a desire to write for and about two women immediate and important to his life and arrived at that goal by creating a play remarkable for its political prescience speaks to how deeply the world lives in him and he in the world. It's as if writing about what he cares about, about that which is dear and close to him, will inevitably give rise to a deeply inquiring articulation of that in which we all live, in the political and social surrounding of our world, now.

The great pleasure I have experienced in coming to know the play more completely since my initial exposure to it in performance has derived precisely from discovering its layers. Certainly it is a political play; it is, as well, a story about a family. Embedded in both of these narratives is, further, an inquiry into language, into the personal and cultural codes of the mother tongue. The play opens with a sustained and virtuosic speech act, and from there moves to a field of speakers who invoke a variety of languages and codes:

Esperanto, the various tribal languages of Afghanistan, English, French, the Dewey Decimal system, Milton's computer languages. It is a veritable tower of Babel (an image that Milton explicitly invokes). The Biblical allusion is resonant: it envisions an original condition in which all people are one and positions their eventual division as a function of their secularism and hubris. Humankind is burdened by the need to express a common condition but without a common language to do so: "Therefore is the name of it called Babel; because the Lord did therefore confound the language of the earth: and from thence did the Lord scatter them abroad upon the face of the Earth." (Genesis 11:9).

Homebody/Kabul is a record of this scattering: a world in which the mother tongue (inscribed in the play as the Homebody: the logorrheic mother) has been lost. Her recovery is violent, uncertain—a displacement more than a restoration. The woman sitting in the parlor of a quiet British home by the play's end—the new homebody—is a foreigner, a woman smuggled out of an indigenous culture determined to destroy her, safe only as a refugee. The ironies are profound: neither woman (the Homebody of the play's opening; Mahala, the Afghan woman in the parlor at the play's end) can give voice to her inner self in her native tongue. No one is "at home" in the play. There exists, instead, a terrible longing to be understood, to touch the authentic (instead of its displacement, its substitute). That, of course, is the engine of language: the signifier that stands in for the signified—the symbol in place of the genuine article. *Homebody/Kabul* is an investigation—set in the language of contemporary politics—into how we might find the bridge, how we might become a traveler across our boundaries (instead of a tourist). Our common language is a polyphony.

Martha Lavey,
Artistic Director, Steppenwolf Theatre Company
July 2003

ACKNOWLEDGMENTS

Most importantly, Nancy Hatch Dupree gave me her kind permission to use several sections and sentences from *An Historical Guide to Kabul*, altered to suit my purposes, in the Homebody's monologue. Ms. Dupree's elegant prose, dazzling erudition and deep love for her subject had a shaping effect not only on the style but also in the substance of *Homebody/Kabul*.

Another valuable collaborator, Nisar Ahmad Zuri, painstakingly translated my lines into Dari and Pashtun, and along the way provided me with invaluable information about Afghanistan.

Alan Edelstein introduced me to Mr. Zuri, and also shared with me his experiences in Kabul. I regret that we never managed to travel there together. I'm grateful to him and to Mike Hsu for introducing me to Alan.

At a rally in support of immigrants' rights in London, in 1998, I met an Iraqi poet, Hussein al-Amily, who showed me his Esperanto poetry. His story inspired one aspect of the character of Khwaja Aziz Mondanabosh.

Annie Castledine was the first director of the monologue, when it was part of a reading series sponsored by the Moving Theatre Company in London; Annie's enthusiasm for what seemed to me, at the moment of just having written it, a strange bit of business, was incredibly helpful and encouraging. Francis Alexander and the folks at the Chelsea Theatre Centre in London gave the monologue its first and second home.

Eve Ensler was similarly generous in sharing tales and photographs of her hair-raising adventures in Afghanistan. Dr. Roger Walzman gave me terminology to use in the dismemberment monologue. Benjamin Levy gave me an explanation of electronic engineering which spoke to the heart of the play. Madeleine George provided the Russian, James Magruder the French, Carl Weber the German for Mahala. Arabic translations were provided by Munir Metwally. Peter Marsden gave me useful information and advice, and his book, *The Taliban*, one of the first on the subject, was my introduction to modern Afghan politics. Professor Deborah Stead improved my definition of recession. Joseph Kamal made an important contribution to Doctor Qari Shah's postmortem, which resulted in its final line. Bill Camp allowed me to incorporate two inspired moments of his performance into the text.

Craig Lucas and Michael Mayer held hands and dispensed sterling dramaturgical advice. Tony Taccone committed Berkeley Rep to a production while he held an unproduceable 250-page script in his hands. Joyce Ketay spent 275,943 hours on the phone listen to me freak out and she never billed me for a single minute. Richard Garmise helped keep *Homebody/Kabul* a musical.

Kimberly T. Flynn was busy during my work on the play trying to save New York City from various eco-catastrophes, but I drew endlessly from our years of exchanges.

Dr. Deborah Glazer is a superb psychoanalyst. The play was written post-termination but its completion should be accounted the proof of the pudding. Framji Minwalla made several superb suggestions for the revision.

My brother Eric, who always insists that I stop whining and get back to writing, held my feet to the fire on an all-important visit to Vienna, where he lives, and where the Kabul section of the play was begun, in the reading room of the Universität Wien. My sister Lesley, whose painting graces the cover of the book, also provided encouragement, advice, artistic and sororal commiseration, and love. We three, our father William, and my devoted aunt Martha, know best and miss most the spirit that haunts the painting and the play.

Without Jim Nicola's insistence, openness, reckless faith, sharp eye, the play would never have been written. Lynn Moffat and the staff and board of New York Theatre Workshop have my gratitude and love. David Esbjornson and Beth Clancy helped me usher the play onto its first stage, the Chelsea Theatre Centre in London. Martha Lavey, artistic director of Steppenwolf Theatre Company, joined me together with Frank Galati for the play's final, tripartite progress. Frank's boundless enthusiasm and willingness to share the rehearsal room with his playwright made it possible to solve certain previously elusive aspects of the text. Through emails and phone calls Bart Sher and I shared insights, questions and rewrites.

The play's own periplum, when it returned to New York in 2004, was made possible by Joe Melillo and his staff at the Brooklyn Academy of Music.

Gordon Davidson supervised my last two years of work on the play, urging me to continue working, giving us a home in Los Angeles and making the transfer back to New York possible.

Mandy Mishell Hackett's contribution as dramaturg to the development of *Homebody/Kabul* can only be described as central.

Linda Emond set new records for patient waiting while I groped about for the rest of the play. Her commitment and talent leave me breathless with admiration, gratitude and guilt.

Maggie Gyllenhaal was always meant to do this play, but it took a while for our collaboration on Priscilla to begin in earnest. *Homebody/Kabul* could not have been completed—if that's the word—without her.

Oskar Eustis agreed to guide the play and the playwright through the straits and narrows; he is my navigator. Long live the plumpes denken geschichtsline!

Mark Harris, my boyfriend/husband/partner/person, provided more indulgence, exhortation, admonition, advice than anyone else, as well as the name of the character Priscilla Ceiling and several truly remarkable insights that transformed the play. He is a lion.

Tita Cahn gave me permission to use her husband's marvelous songs in the play.

Declan Donnellan and Nick Ormerod sailed across the Atlantic to do the play at New York Theatre Workshop. I am grateful for their genius and their spirit of adventure. No one does work I admire more. With all my heart I wish them many triumphs and much joy.

PRODUCTION HISTORY

Homebody was first performed as a staged reading at the Chelsea Theatre Centre in London in December 1997. It was directed by Annie Castledine. The role of the Homebody was performed by Kika Markham.

Homebody received its first full production at the Chelsea Theatre Centre in July 1999. It was directed by David Esbjornson, with costumes by Beth Clancy. The role of the Homebody was performed by Kika Markham.

Homebody/Kabul premiered at New York Theatre Workshop (James C. Nicola, Artistic Director; Lynn Moffat, Managing Director) in New York City on December 19, 2001. It was directed by Declan Donnellan, with design by Nick Ormerod, lights by Brian MacDevitt, sound by Dan Moses Schreier, movement direction by Barbara Karger, dramaturgy by Oscar Eustis and Mandy Mishell Hackett, dialect coaching by Deborah Hecht and Gillian Lane-Plescia, cultural/language consulting by Nisar Ahmad Zuri, and production stage management by Martha Donaldson.

THE HOMEBODY	Linda Emond
DOCTOR QARI SHAH	Joseph Kamal
MULLAH AFTAR ALI DURRANNI	Firdous Bamji

MILTON CEILING	Dylan Baker
QUANGO TWISTLETON	Bill Camp
PRISCILLA CEILING	Kelly Hutchinson
LADY IN BURQA	Rita Wolf
THE MUNKRAT	Dariush Kashani
KHWAJA AZIZ MONDANABOSH	Yusef Bulos
ZAI GARSHI	Sean T. Krishnan
MAHALA	Rita Wolf
THE MARABOUT	Sean T. Krishnan
A BORDER GUARD	Jay Charan

Homebody/Kabul opened at Trinity Repertory Company (Oskar Eustis, Artistic Director; Edgar Dobie, Managing Director) in Providence, Rhode Island, on March 15, 2002. It was directed by Oskar Eustis, with sets by Eugene Lee, lights by Deb Sullivan, sound by Peter Sasha Hurowitz, costumes by William Lane, dramaturgy by Oscar Eustis and Mandy Mishell Hackett, stage management by Jennifer Sturch and production stage management by Ruth E. Sternberg.

THE HOMEBODY	Anne Scurria
DOCTOR QARI SHAH	Demosthenes Chrysan
MULLAH AFTAR ALI DURRANNI	Donnie Keshawarz
MILTON CEILING	Brian McEleney
QUANGO TWISTLETON	Stephen Thorne
PRISCILLA CEILING	Angela Brazil
LADY IN BURQA	Yolande Bavan
THE MUNKRAT	Omar Metwally
KHWAJA AZIZ MONDANABOSH	Apollo Dukakis
ZAI GARSHI	Deep Katdare
MAHALA	Yolande Bavan
THE MARABOUT	Omar Metwally
A BORDER GUARD	Omar Metwally

Homebody/Kabul was produced by Berkeley Repertory Theatre (Tony Taccone, Artistic Director; Susan Medak, Managing Director) in Berkeley, California, on April 19, 2002. It was directed by Tony Taccone, with scenic design by Kate Edmunds, lights by Peter Maradudin, sound by Matthew Spiro, original score by Paul Godwin, costumes by Lydia Tanji, production dramaturgy by Luan Schooler, script dramaturgy by Oskar Eustis and Mandy Michelle Hackett, dialect coaching by Lynne Soffer, and stage management by Michael Suenkel (April 19 to June 23) and Shona Mitchell (June 25 to July 14).

THE HOMEBODY	Michelle Morain
DOCTOR QARI SHAH/THE MARABOUT	Julian López-Morillas
MULLAH AFTAR ALI DURRANNI	Hector Correa
MILTON CEILING	Charles Shaw Robinson
QUANGO TWISTLETON	Bruce McKenzie (April 19 to June 9)
QUANGO TWISTLETON	Rod Gnapp (June 11 to July 14)
PRISCILLA CEILING	Heidi Dippold
THE MUNKRAT/A BORDER GUARD	Rahul Gupta
KHWAJA AZIZ MONDANABOSH	Harsh Nayyar
ZAI GARSHI	Waleed Zuaiter
MAHALA	Jacqueline Antaramian

The play was produced at The Young Vic (David Lan, Artistic Director; Kevin Fitzmaurice, Executive Director; in association with Cheek by Jowl and New York Theatre Workshop) in London on May 10, 2002. It was directed by Declan Donnellan, with design by Nick Ormerod, lights by Judith Greenwood, sound by Paul Arditti, music by Paddy Cunneen, costumes by Lydia Tanji, costume supervision by Angie Burns, movement by Jane Gibson, stage management by Suzi Blakey and company stage management by Jules Evans.

THE HOMEBODY/LADY IN BURQA	Kika Markham
DOCTOR QARI SHAH/A BORDER GUARD	Antony Bunsee
MULLAH AFTAR ALI DURRANNI	Kevork Malikyan
MILTON CEILING	William Chubb
QUANGO TWISTLETON	Mark Bazeley
PRISCILLA CEILING	Jacqueline Defferary
THE MUNKRAT/A BORDER GUARD	Rahul Gupta
KHWAJA AZIZ MONDANABOSH	Nadim Sawalha
ZAI GARSHI/A MUNKRAT/THE MARABOUT	Silas Carson
MAHALA/ LADY IN BURQA	Souad Faress

The play was produced at Steppenwolf Theatre Company (Martha Lavey, Artistic Director; David Hawkanson, Executive Director; in association with The Center Theatre Group/ Mark Taper Forum) in Chicago, Illinois, on July 20, 2003. It was directed by Frank Galati, with set design by James Schuette, lights by Christopher Akerlind, sound by Joe Cerqua, costumes by Mara Blumenfeld, dialect coaching by Linda Gates and stage management by Robert H. Satterlee.

THE HOMEBODY	Amy Morton
DOCTOR QARI SHAH	Ali Farahnakian
MULLAH AFTAR ALI DURRANNI	Aasif Mandvi
MILTON CEILING	Reed Birney
QUANGO TWISTLETON	Tracy Letts
PRISCILLA CEILING	Elizabeth Ledo
THE MUNKRAT/A BORDER GUARD	Arian Moayed
KHWAJA AZIZ MONDANABOSH	Firdous Bamji
ZAI GARSHI	Omar Metwally
MAHALA/ LADY IN BURQA	Diana Simonzadeh
SUPERNUMERARIES	Jeremy Beiler, Diana M. Konopka, Raymond Kurut, Chris Yonan

The play was produced at Intiman Theatre (Bartlett Sher, Artistic Director; Laura Penn, Managing Director) in Seattle, Washington, on September 17, 2003. It was directed by Bartlett Sher, with scenic design by John Arnone, lights by Justin Townsend, sound by Peter John Still, costumes by Elizabeth Caitlin Ward, dialect/language coaching by Judith Shahn, dramaturgy by Mame Hunt and stage management by Wendiana Walker. New York casting was by Janet Foster.

THE HOMEBODY	Ellen McLaughlin
DOCTOR QARI SHAH/THE MUNKRAT/	
A BORDER GUARD	Shanga Parker
MULLAH AFTAR ALI DURRANNI/ZAI GARSHI	Ed Chemaly
MILTON CEILING	Laurence Ballard
QUANGO TWISTLETON	Simeon Moore
PRISCILLA CEILING	Kristin Flanders
KHWAJA AZIZ MONDANABOSH	Ismail Bashey
MAHALA	Jacqueline Antaramian
ENSEMBLE	Zaki Abdelhamid, Onkar Meno Sharma

The play was produced at The Center Theatre Group/Mark Taper Forum (Gordon Davidson, Artistic Director; Charles Dillingham, Managing Director; in association with Steppenwolf Theatre Center) in Los Angeles, California on October 2, 2003. It was directed by Frank Galati, with set design by James Schuette, lights by Chris Akerlind, sound by Joe Cerqua, costumes by Mara Blumenfeld, dialect coaching by Farzana Hakimi, and production stage management by Jimmie McDermott.

THE HOMEBODY	Linda Emond
DOCTOR QARI SHAH	Maz Jobrani
MULLAH AFTAR ALI DURRANNI	Aasif Mandvi
MILTON CEILING	Reed Birney
QUANGO TWISTLETON	Bill Camp

PRISCILLA CEILING	Maggie Gyllenhaal
THE MUNKRAT/A BORDER GUARD	Rahul Gupta
KHWAJA AZIZ MONDANABOSH	Firdous Bamji
ZAI GARSHI	Dariush Kashani
MAHALA/LADY IN BURQA	Rita Wolf
SUPERNUMERARIES	Mueen Jahan Ahmad, Gillian Doyle, Laura Kachergus, John Rafter Lee, Kamal Maray, Shaheen Vaaz

The play was presented by Brooklyn Academy of Music, The Center Theatre Group/Mark Taper Forum and Steppenwolf Theatre Company at BAM's Harvey Theatre in Brooklyn, New York, in May 2004. It was directed by Frank Galati, with set design by James Schuette, lights by Chris Akerlind, sound and original composition by Joe Cerqua, and costumes by Mara Blumenfeld.

THE HOMEBODY	Linda Emond
DOCTOR QARI SHAH	Ali Reza
MULLAH AFTAR ALI DURRANNI	Aasif Mandvi
MILTON CEILING	Reed Birney
QUANGO TWISTLETON	Bill Camp
PRISCILLA CEILING	Maggie Gyllenhaal
THE MUNKRAT/A BORDER GUARD	Rahul Gupta
KHWAJA AZIZ MONDANABOSH	Firdous Bamji
ZAI GARSHI	Dariush Kashani
MAHALA	Rita Wolf
SUPERNUMERARIES	Mueen Jahan Ahmad, Gillian Doyle, Laura Kachergus, John Rafter Lee, Kamal Maray, Shaheen Vaaz

HOMEBODY/KABUL

CAST

THE HOMEBODY
British woman in her mid-forties.

DOCTOR QARI SHAH
Pashtun Afghan man in his forties/fifties, a doctor.

MULLAH AFTAR ALI DURRANNI
Pashtun Afghan man in his forties/fifties, Taliban minister.

MILTON CEILING
British man in his early forties, computer specialist,
husband of the Homebody.

QUANGO TWISTLETON
British man, mid-to-late twenties/early thirties, aid worker,
unofficial liaison for the British government in Kabul.

PRISCILLA CEILING
British woman in her early twenties, unemployed, adrift,
daughter of Milton and the Homebody.

AFGHAN WOMAN
Any age.

THE MUNKRAT
Pashtun Afghan man, twenties, with the Nai Azz Munkar,
Taliban religious police.

KHWAJA AZIZ MONDANABOSH
Tajik Afghan man, thirties/early forties, a poet and mahram
(male escort/guide for women).

ZAI GARSHI
Afghan man, thirties/forties, a former actor, now sells hats.

MAHALA
Pashtun Afghan woman, late forties/early fifties,
before the Taliban arrived, a librarian.

A BORDER GUARD
Pashtun Afghan man, Taliban, twenties/thirties.

SETTING

The play takes place in London, England and Kabul, Afghanistan just before and just after the American bombardment of the suspected terrorist training camps in Khost, Afghanistan, August 1998.

The final scene, Periplum, is set in London in the spring of 1999.

NOTES

A Note for the Homebody:

When the Homebody, in Act One, Scene 1, refers to the street on which she found the hat shop, she doesn't mention its name; instead, where the name would fall in the sentence, she makes a wide, sweeping gesture in the air with her right hand, from left to right, almost as if to say: "I know the name but I will not tell you." It is the same gesture each time.

In the Play:

A sentence ending with a "..." indicates that the speaker has trailed off...

A sentence ending with a "—" indicates that the speaker is interrupted by someone or something.

Among the many challenges regarding pronunciation presented by the script, it feels silly to make a special point of three in particular; nevertheless I feel compelled to note that the surname of Pelham Grenville Wodehouse (1881–1975) is pronounced "Woodhouse," Reuters is pronounced "Royters," and in Act Two, Scene 5, when Mahala uses the word "projectile," it should be pronounced as per the French "projhecteel."

In Act Two, Scene 4, Zai Garshi *recites* the Sinatra lyrics, he shouldn't sing them.

I have received inquiries from theaters wishing to do only Act One, Scene 1, the Homebody monologue. I resisted agreeing to this while working on the play, but I no longer have any objections—though obviously I would rather the entire play be produced.

The shape of the map of present-day Afghanistan resembles a left-hand fist with the thumb open.

—NABI MISDAQ, *AHMAD SHAH DURRANI 1722–1772*

It is more appropriate to consider Afghanistan as a place of enormous complexity that has been subject to a constant state of flux throughout history rather than to view it as somehow caught in a time-warp, with life going on as it has always done.

—PETER MARSDEN, *THE TALIBAN*

Afghanistan lies at the crossroads of South and Central Asia; its northern plains an extension of the steppes to Turkmenistan, the Hindu Kush mountains an adjunct to the Himalayas, its southern deserts a prelude to the Persian Gulf. Linguistically, culturally and ethnically Afghanistan's northern Uzbeks, Turkmen and Tajiks look northwards to Central Asia, the centrally located Hazaras look westwards to Iran, and the southern and eastern Pashtuns and Baluch find more resonance in the east in Pakistan. Although distinct from them, each group and region has more in common with its neighbors over the border than with each other.

—CHRIS BOWERS, "A BRIEF HISTORY OF AFGHANISTAN," FROM *ESSENTIAL FIELD GUIDE TO AFGHANISTAN*

"Periplum" is Pound's shorthand for a tour which takes you round then back again. And such a tour is by definition profitable, if not in coins then in knowledge.

—HUGH KENNER, *THE ELSEWHERE COMMUNITY*

These examples should teach you the way to treat hearts . . . The general technique consists in doing the opposite of everything the soul inclines to and craves. God (Exalted is He!) has summed up all these things in His statement: "And whoever fears the standing before his Lord, and forbids his soul its whim, for him Heaven shall be the place of resort."

—AL-GHAZALI, *ON DISCIPLING THE SOUL AND BREAKING THE TWO DESIRES*

The world had been destroyed several times before the creation of man.

—LORD BYRON, *CAIN*

In Washington, Pentagon officials said that a U.S. warplane missed a Taliban military target at Kabul airport and that a 2,000 pound bomb the plane was carrying apparently struck a residential neighborhood.

At the scene of the hit, one man sat in his wheelchair, weeping next to a pile of rubble where his house once stood. Other residents wandered about in a daze.

"We lost everything, our house and property," one woman said. "We are so afraid of the attacks we have forgotten our own names and can't even understand what we say to each other."

—*NEW YORK TIMES*, OCTOBER 13, 2001

Act One

SCENE 1

A woman is sitting on a plain wooden chair next to a table in the kitchen of her home in London. There's a lamp on the table, and perhaps the table is covered with a homey, simple oilcloth.
There's another chair at the opposing end of the table; a coat has been neatly folded across the back of this chair, and a pocketbook is on the chair seat.
On the floor near her chair, a shopping bag.
She is reading from a small book:

THE HOMEBODY
"Our story begins at the very dawn of history, circa 3,000 B.C. . . ."
(Interrupting herself:)
I am reading from an outdated guidebook about the city of Kabul. In Afghanistan. In the valleys of the Hindu Kush mountains. A guidebook to a city which as we all know, has . . . undergone change.
My reading, my research is moth-like. Impassioned, fluttery, doomed. A subject strikes my fancy: Kabul—you will see why, that's the tale I'm telling—but then, I can't help myself, it's almost perverse, in libraries, in secondhand bookshops, I invariably seek out not the source but all that which was dropped by the wayside on the way to the source, outdated

guidebooks—this was published in 1965, and it is now 1998, so the book is a vestige superannuated by some . . . thirty-three years, long enough for Christ to have been born and die on the cross—old magazines, hysterical political treatises written by an advocate of some long-since defeated or abandoned or transmuted cause; and I find these irrelevant and irresistible, ghostly, dreamy, the knowing what *was* known before the more that has since become known overwhelms . . . As we are, many of us, overwhelmed, and succumbing to luxury . . .

(She reads from the guidebook:)
"Our story begins at the very dawn of history, circa 3,000 B.C., when the Aryans, not in armies but in family groups, traveled south from beyond the River Oxus, to cross the Hindu Kush mountains on their way to northern India. This crossing must have made a great impression for, nearly two thousand years later, when the Rigveda, the great hymnic epic poem of the Aryan peoples, is written down, several verses retain the memory of the serene beauty of the valleys of the Kabul River."

(She looks up from the guidebook)
Several months ago I was feeling low and decided to throw a party and a party needs festive hats. So I took the tube to _____, *(She gestures; see prefatory "Notes")* where there are shops full of merchandise from exotic locales, wonderful things made by people who believe, as I do not, as *we* do not, in magic; or who used to believe in magic, and not so long ago, whose grandparents believed in magic, believed that some combination of piety, joy, ecstasy, industry, brought to bear on the proper raw materials, wood for instance known to be the favored nesting place of a certain animus or anima possessed of powers released, enlisted in beneficent ways towards beneficent ends when carved, adorned, adored just so . . . before colonization and the savage stripping away of such beliefs. For magic beliefs are immensely strong, I think, only if their essential fragility is respected. It's a paradox. If such beliefs, magic beliefs, are untouched, they endure. And

who knows? Work magic, perhaps. If they are untouched; and that is hard, for such is the expansive nature of these times that every animate and inanimate thing, corporeal or incorporeal, actual or ideational, real or imagined, every, every discrete unit of . . . of *being*: if a thing can be said to *be*, to *exist*, then such is the nature of these expansive times that this thing which is must suffer to be *touched*. Ours is a time of connection; the private, and we must accept this, and it's a hard thing to accept, the private is *gone*. All must be touched. All touch corrupts. All must be corrupted. And if you're thinking how awful these sentiments are, you are perfectly correct, these are awful times, but you must remember as well that *this* has always been the chiefest characteristic of the Present, to everyone living through it; always, throughout history, and so far as I can see for all the days and years to come until the sun and the stars fall down and the clocks have all ground themselves to expiry and the future has long long shaded away into Time Immemorial: the Present is *always* an awful place to be. And it remains awful to us, the scene of our crime, the place of our shame, for at least Oh, let's say three full decades of recession—by which word, recession, I am to be taken to mean recedence, not recession as in two consecutive quarters of negative growth in gross domestic product. For a three-decades regnum of imperceptible but mercifully implacable recedency we shudder to recall the times through which we have lived, the Recent Past, about which no one wants to think; and then, have you noticed? Even the most notorious decade three or four decades later is illumined from within. Some light inside is switched on. The scenery becomes translucent, beautifully lit; features of the landscape glow; the shadows are full of agreeable color. Cynics will attribute this transformation to senescence and nostalgia; I who am optimistic, have you noticed? attribute this inner illumination to understanding. It is wisdom's hand which switches on the light within. Ah, now I see what that was all about. Ah, now, now I see why we suffered so back then, now I see what we went through. I understand.

(She reads from the guidebook:)
"Nothing is known of the Aryan passage through the valleys of the Hindu Kush, no writing or significant structure remains from the Aryan settlements which undoubtedly existed on the banks of the Kabul River, one of which would eventually grow into the city of Kabul. The first contemporaneous account to mention the city is recorded circa 520 B.C., when Darius the Great, Achaemenid Persian conqueror and builder of Persepolis, annexed twenty-nine countries to the Persian empire, parts of India, all of what we now know as Afghanistan, including the Kabul Valley. In the summer of 329 B.C., Alexander the Macedonian, having trampled the Achaemenid imperium in his victorious march through Persia, makes camp in the Hindu Kush city of Khandahar, and orders the building of the city of Alexandria-ad-Caucasum."
(She looks up from the guidebook)
Oh I love the world! I love love love love the world! Having said so much, may I assume most of you will have dismissed me as a simpleton? I cannot hope to contravene your peremptory low estimation, which may for all its peremptoriness nevertheless be exactly appropriate. I live with the world's mild censure, or would do were it the case that I ever strayed far enough from my modesty, or should I say my essential surfeit of inconsequence, to so far attract the world's attention as to provoke from it its mild censure; but I have never strayed so far from the unlit to the spotlight, and so should say rather that I live with the world's utter indifference, which I have always taken to be a form of censure-in-potentia.

I speak . . . I can't help myself. Elliptically. Discursively. I've read too many books, and that's not boasting, for I haven't read *many* books, but I've read too many, exceeding I think my capacity for syncresis—is that a word?—straying rather into synchisis, which is a word. So my diction, my syntax, well, it's so *irritating*, I apologize, I do, it's very hard, I know.

To listen. I blame it on the books, how else to explain it? My parents don't speak like this; no one I know does; no one does. It's an *alien influence*, and my borders have only ever been broached by books. Sad to say.

Only ever been broached by books. Except once, briefly. Which is I suppose the tale I'm telling, or rather, trying to tell.

You must be patient. There is an old Afghan saying, which, in rough translation, from the Farsi, goes: *"The man who has patience has roses. The man who has no patience has no trousers."* I am not fluent in Farsi, of course, I read this, and as I say it must be a rough translation.

(She reads from the guidebook:)

"Alexander the Great summoned to the Kabul Valley a mighty army comprising tens of thousands of soldiers from Egypt, Persia, and Central Asia and went on to conquer India. When Alexander's own troops grew weary of battle, in 325 B.C., they forced their commander to desist from further conquest. Alexander died in 323 B.C., just as he was planning a return to the Hindu Kush to oversee the Grecianization of this most remarkable land."

(She pauses her reading)

My husband cannot bear my . . . the sound of me and has threatened to leave on this account and so I rarely speak to him anymore. We both take powerful antidepressants. His pills have one name and mine another. I frequently take his pills instead of mine so I can know what he's feeling. I keep mine in a glass bowl next to the bathroom sink, a nice wide-mouthed bowl, very wide, wide open, like an epergne, but so far as I know he never takes my pills but ingests only his own, which are yellow and red, while mine are green and creamy-white; and I find his refusal to sample dull. A little dull.

(She resumes, from the guidebook:)

"By 322 B.C., only a year after Alexander's death, his vast Macedonian empire had disassembled. Herodotus tells us that the hill tribes of the Kabul Valley were among the first

and the most ferocious in rejecting Macedonian authority. Seleucus Nicator, Alexander's successor in the east, attempted to regain the Hindu Kush but was daunted when he encountered, in 305 B.C., in the passes of the Hindu Kush, the armed forces of the Maurya Dynasty which had come to rule India. In exchange for the hand of the daughter of the Maurya emperor, Chandragupta, and for five hundred elephants, the Kabul Valley passed for the first time under Indian suzerainty."
(She puts the guidebook down)
A party needs hats. I had no hope that this would be a good party. My parties are never good parties. This party was intended to celebrate my husband's having completed some joyless task at his place of business, which has something to do with the routing of multiplēe expressive electronic tone signals at extraordinary speeds across millions upon millions of kilometers of wire and cable and fiber and space; I understand none of it and indeed it's quite impossible imagining my husband having to do in any real way with processes so . . . speedy, myriad, nervous, miraculous. But that parti-colored cloud of gas there, in that galaxy there so far away, that cloud there so hot and blistered by clustering stars, exhaling protean scads of infinitely irreducible fiery data in the form of energy pulses and streams of slicing, shearing, unseeable light—does that nebula know it nebulates? Most likely not. So my husband. It knows nothing, its *nature* is to stellate and constellate and nebulate and add its heft and vortices and frequencies to the Universal Drift, un-self-consciously effusing, effusing, gaseously effusing, and so my husband, and so not I, who seem forever to be imploding and collapsing and am incapable it would seem of lending even this simple tale to the Universal Drift, of telling this simple tale without supersaturating my narrative with maddeningly infuriating or more probably irritating synchitic epexegeses.
Synchitic epexegeses. Jesus.
A party needs hats and in my mind's eye I remembered quite remarkable hats, not as tall as fezzes nor yet as closely cleav-

ing to the curve of the skull as a skullcap, but really rather
pillboxy as ladies wore hats in the early '60s; but these
mind's-eye hats were made of tough brilliant dyed wools and
scraps of elaborate geometrically arabesqued carpet into
which sequins and diamantines and carbuncles and glassene
beading had been sewn to dazzling, charming premodern
effect. I could see these hats perched on top of the heads of
the family members and friends who usually appear at my
parties, lovely lovely people all of them but when we assem-
ble we rather . . . affect one another, one might even say
afflict one another, in baleful ways and tend to dampen one
another's festive spirits, there's no . . . I suppose one would
like something combustible at a party, something catalytic,
some fizz, each element triggering transformation in all the
other elements till all elements, which is to say, *guests*, are . . .
surprising to themselves and return home feeling less, less
certain of, of those *certainties* which . . . *Because* of which,
for example, powerful antidepressants are consumed.
(She reads from the guidebook:)
"The third century B.C. was a prosperous time for the Kabul
Valley, situated midway between the empires of the Seleu-
cids and the Mauryas, profiting thusly from an extensive
trade with both which must have included furs from Central
Asia and a recent discovery of the Chinese, silk. By the end
of the third century the far-flung Mauryan empire had disappeared and a period of disorder, migration and tribal unrest
follows, for which the records are clouded and confused."
(She looks up from the guidebook)
My antidepressant is called . . . something, a made-up word,
a portmanteau chemical cocktail word confected by punning
psychopharmacologists but I can never remember precisely
what to ask for when I . . . My husband explains to me with
bitter impacted patience each time I request it of him the
workings of . . . Ameliorate-za-pozulac, its workings upon
my brain; I cannot retain his bitter impacted explanation,
but I believe it's all to do with salt somehow. I believe in fact

this drug is a kind of talented salt. And so I imagine my brain floating in a salt bath, frosted with a rime of salt, a pickle-brine brain, pink-beige walnut-wrinkled nutmeat within a crystalliform quartzoid ice-white hoarfrost casing, a gemmy shell, gemmiparous: budding. How any of this is meant to counteract depression is more than I can say.

Perhaps it is the sufficient pleasing image which cheers one and makes life's burdens less difficult to bear.

(She reads from the guidebook:)

"In the middle of the second century B.C., during the Greco-Bactrian confusion, a Chinese tribe, the Hsiung-Nu, attacked a rival tribe, the Yueh-Chih, and drove them from their homes to what is now southern Afghanistan. Then the Hsiung-Nu, displaced from their new homes by another Chinese tribe, also migrated to Afghanistan and once again displaced the Yueh-Chih, who emigrated to the Kabul Valley. As the first century B.C. dawns, the Valley, populated by Indo-Greeks, Mauryas and Macedonians, is now surrounded by the restless nomadic kingdoms of the Yueh-Chih.

"By 48 B.C. the Chinese tribes are united under the banner of their largest clan, the Kushans. From the city of Kapisa, the Kushan court came to rival the Caesars in Rome." And I'd never *heard* of the Kushans, have you? Nor for that matter the Greco-Bactrian Confusion! Though it *feels* familiar, does it not, the Greco-Bactrian Confusion? When did it end? The guidebook does not relate. *Did* it end? Are we perhaps still in it? Still *in* the Greco-Bactrian Confusion? Would it surprise you, really, to learn that we are? Don't you feel it would I don't know *explain* certain things? "Ah yes it is hard I know, to *understand* but you see it's the Greco-Bactrian Confusion, which no one ever actually bothered clearing up, and, well here we are."

But let us return to the Kushans:

"From the city of Kapisa, the Kushan court came to rival the Caesars in Rome. Buddhism, Hinduism, Grecian and Persian deities are gathered into the valleys of the Hindu Kush where a remarkable cross-fertilization takes place."

16

(She puts the guidebook down)
In my mind's eye, yet from memory: I had seen these abbreviated fezlike pillboxy attenuated yarmulkite millinarisms, um, *hats*, I'm sorry I *will* try to stop, *hats*, yes, in a crowded shop on _____ *(Gesture)* which I must have passed and mentally noted on my way towards God knows what, who cares, a dusty shop crowded with artifacts, relics, remnants, little . . . doodahs of a culture once aswarm with spirit matter, radiant with potent magic, the disenchanted dull detritus of which has washed up upon our culpable shores, its magic now shriveled into the safe container of *aesthetic*, which is to say, *consumer* appeal. You know, Third World junk. As I remember, as my mind's eye saw, through its salt crust, Afghan junk. That which was once Afghan, which we, having waved our credit cards in its general direction, have made into junk.

I remembered the shop, where I thought it was, what its windows were like, sure I'd never find it again and yet there it was in my mind's eye and I traveled to the spot my mind's eye had fixed upon and I was correct! Took the tube, chewed my nails, there was the shop! Precisely as my salt-wounded mind's eye's corneal rotogravured sorry sorry. I found the shop. It was run by Afghan refugees.

And here are the hats. There are ten. They cost three ninety-nine each.

(She displays the hats, removing them one by one from the shopping bag and putting them on the table)
Looking at the hat we imagine not bygone days of magic belief but the suffering behind the craft. This century has taught us to direct our imagination however fleetingly toward the hidden suffering: evil consequence of evil action taken long ago, conjoining with relatively recent wickedness and wickedness perpetuated now, in August 1998, now now now, even as I speak and speak and speak. But whether the product of starveling-manned sweatshop or remote not-on-the-grid village, poor yet still resisting the onslaught of

modernity, touched, of course, yet not, though it is only a matter of time, isn't it? not corrupted; whether removed from the maker by the middleman to the merchant by filch or swindle or gunpoint or even murder; whether, for that matter, even Afghan in origin; and not Pakistani; or Peruvian; if not in point of fact made in London by children, aunts and elderly uncles in the third-floor flat above the shop on _____ *(Gesture):* The hats are beautiful; relatively inexpensive; sinister if you've a mind to see them that way; and sad. As dislocations are. And marvelous, as dislocations are. Always bloody.

This one is particularly nice.

(She puts a hat on her head, and reads from the guidebook:)

"Severe economic crises throughout the region in the second century A.D. made it easy for the Sassanians, a purely Iranian Persian dynasty, to claim the Hindu Kush Valley as a semi-independent satrapy. The inhabitants of Kabul from the Kushano-Sassanian period appear to have remained Buddhist, while their Sassanian overlords were obstreperous worshipers of Zoroaster." *(She looks up from the book)* "Obstreperous worshipers of Zoroaster"! For that phrase alone I deem this book a worthy addition to my pickpenny library of remaindered antilegomenoi. *(Back to the book)* "Sassanian hegemony—" *(Up from the book)* Antilegomenoi are volumes of castoff or forgotten knowledge, in case you were wondering. *(Back to the book)* "Sassanian hegemony was toppled by the Hephthalites, or white Huns, who commenced a reign of legendary destructiveness around 400 A.D., savagely persecuting the indigenous worship of Buddha—Buddhism having found many adherents among Hindu Kush peoples as its monks carried news of the Buddha from India through Afghanistan to China. Apart from their fabled viciousness, almost nothing is known about the Hephthalites."

(She looks up from the guidebook)

Nothing when this book was written, and it is rather old. Perhaps more is known now, though archaeology in the area has

been interrupted. Very little digging, except recently, did you read this, the bodies of two thousand Taliban soldiers were found in a mass grave in northern Afghanistan, prisoners who were executed, apparently by soldiers loyal to the overthrown government of Burhanuddin Rabbani. So someone is digging, and perhaps more now is known about the Hephthalites.
(She reads from the guidebook:)
"Hephthalite rule ended in 531 A.D. after which a state of anarchy prevailed over the entire region, each town protected by an independent chieftain, and the remaining Hephthalite princes—" who, you will remember, made their appearance just one paragraph previous, razing Buddhist temples—"the remaining Hephthalite princes having by this time *converted to Buddhism.*"
And made a great vulgar noise about it, I shouldn't wonder. I find myself disliking intensely the Hephthalites.
"Meanwhile, in 642, the banner of Islam"—Islam at last!— "carried forth from the deserts of Arabia, halted its eastern progress when its armies tried to penetrate the heart of what is now Afghanistan; for every hill and town was defended by fierce tribal warriors. Several hundred years were to pass before Kabul would fully surrender to Islam."
(Turning pages, summarizing:)
This brings us to the end of the millennium, 1023. Kabul over the next three or four hundred years will be conquered by first this empire builder and then that one. Genghis Khan swam through the area on a river of blood. The Great Tamurlaine, a Timurid, wounded his foot during a battle near Kabul, says the guidebook, and whatever it was he was named before (the book is not helpful on this) he was henceforth and forevermore known as Timur-I-Lang, Timur Who Limps. Timur-I-Lang, Tamurlaine. Kabul re-baptised him.
(She puts the guidebook down)
And this is what happened, and it's all there is to my little tale, really:
(Accelerate! Quickly:)

The hats were in a barrel which could be seen through the window; puppets hung from the ceiling, carved freestanding figurines, demiurges, attributes, symbols, carven abstractions representing metaphysical principles critical to the governance of perfect cosmologies now lost to all or almost all human memory; amber beads big as your baby's fists, armor plates like pangolin scales strung on thick ropey catgut cordage meant to be worn by rather large rather ferocious men, one would imagine, or who knows; hideous masks with great tusks and lolling tongues and more eyes than are usual, mind's eyes I suppose, and revolving wire racks filled with postcards depicting the severed heads of the Queen and Tony Blair, well not *severed* necessarily but with no body appended; Glaswegian *A to Zed Guides* and newspapers in Arabic, in Urdu, in Pushtu, videocassettes of rock balladeers from Benares: well why go on and on, sorry I'm sorry, we've all been in these sorts of shops, no bigger than from here to there, haven't we?

As if

(A bit slower!)

a many-cameled caravan, having roamed across the entire postcolonial not-yet-developed world, crossing the borders of the rainforested kingdoms of Kwashiorkor and Rickets and Untreated Gum Disease and High Infant Mortality Rates, gathering with desperate indiscriminateness—is that the word?—on the mudpitted unpaved trade route its bits and boodle, had finally beached its great heavy no longer portable self in a narrow coal-scuttle of a shop on _____ *(Gesture)*, here, here, caravanseraied here, in the developed and overdeveloped and over-overdeveloped paved wasted now deliquescent post-First World postmodern city of London; all the camels having flopped and toppled and fallen here and died of exhaustion, of shock, of the heartache of refugees, the goods simply piled high upon their dromedary bones, just where they came to rest, and set up shop atop the carcasses, and so on.

I select ten hats, thread my way through the musty heaps of swag and thrownaway and offcast and godforsaken sorry sorry through the merchandise to the counter where a man, an Afghan man, my age I think, perhaps a bit older, stands smiling eager to ring up my purchases and make an imprint of my credit card, and as I hand the card to him I see that three fingers on his right hand have been hacked off, following the line of a perfect clean diagonal from middle, to ring, to little finger, which, the last of the three fingers in the diagonal cut's descent, by, um, hatchet blade? was hewn off almost completely—like this, you see?

(She demonstrates, holding up her hand with the middle, ring and little finger folded down)

But a clean line, you see, not an accident, a measured surgical cut, but not surgery as we know it for what possible medicinal purpose might be served? I tried, as one does, not to register shock, or morbid fascination, as one does my eyes unfocused my senses fled startled to the roof of my skull and then off into the ether like a rapid vapor indifferent to the obstacle of my cranium WHOOSH, clean slate, tabula rasa, terra incognita, where am I yet still my mind's eye somehow continuing to record and detail that poor ruined hand slipping my MasterCard into the . . . you know, that thing, that roller press thing which is used to . . . Never mind. Here, in London, that poor ruined hand.

Imagine.

I know nothing of this hand, its history, of course, nothing.

I did know, well I have learnt since through research that Kabul, which is the ancient capital of Afghanistan, and where once the summer pavilion of Amir Abdur Rahman stood shaded beneath two splendid old chinar trees, beloved of the Moghuls, Kabul, substantial portions of which are now great heaps of rubble, was it was claimed by the Moghul Emperor Babur founded by none other than Cain himself. Biblical Cain. Who is said to be buried in Kabul, in the gardens south of Bala-Hissar in the cemetery known as Shohada-I-Salehin.

I should like to see that. The Grave of Cain. Murder's Grave. Would you eat a potato plucked from *that* soil?

(She reads from the guidebook:)

"The mighty Moghul emperors, who came to rule the Hindu Kush and all of India, adored Kabul and magnified and exalted it. By the eighteenth century the Moghuls, ruling from Delhi and Agra, succumbed to luxury"—that's what it says, they "succumbed to luxury." "Modern Afghanistan is born when, in 1747, heretofore warring Afghan tribal chiefs forge for themselves a state, proclaiming Ahmed Shah Durrani, age twenty-five, King of the Afghans."

(She looks up from the guidebook)

And so the Great Game begins. The Russians seize Kazakhstan, the British seize India, Persia caves in to the Russians, the first Anglo-Afghan war is fought, the bazaar in Kabul is burnt and many many people die, Russia seizes Bokhara, the second Anglo-Afghan war, the First World War, the October Revolution, the third Anglo-Afghan war, also known as the Afghanistan War of Independence, Afghanistan sovereignty first recognized by the Soviet Union in 1921, followed by aid received from the Soviet Union, followed by much of the rest of the twentieth century. Afghanistan is armed by the U.S.S.R. against the Pakistanis, the U.S. refuses assistance, militant Islamic movements form the seed of what will become the Mujahideen, the U.S. begins sending money. Much civil strife, approaching at times a state of civil war, reaction against liberal reforms such as the unveiling of and equal rights for women, democratic elections held, martial law imposed, the Soviet Union invades, the Mujahideen are armed, at first insufficiently, then rather handsomely by the U.S., staggering amounts of firepower, some captured from the Soviets, some purchased, some given by the West, missiles and anti-aircraft cannon and etc. etc. The Soviets for ten years do their best to outdo the Hephthalites in savagery, in barbarism, then like so many other empires traversing the Hindu Kush the U.S.S.R. is swept away, and now the Taliban, and . . .

Well.

(She closes the guidebook and puts it down)
Afghanistan is one of the poorest countries in the world. With one of the world's most decimated infrastructures. No tourism. Who in the world would wish to travel there? In Afghanistan today I would be shrouded entirely in a *burqa*, I should be subject to *hejab*, I should live in terror of the *sharia hudud*, or more probably dead, unregenerate chatterer that I am.

While I am signing the credit card receipt I realize all of a sudden I am able to speak perfect Pushtu, and I ask the man, who I now notice is very beautiful, not on account of regularity of features or smoothness of the skin, no, his skin is broken by webs of lines inscribed by hardships, siroccos and strife, battle scars, perhaps, well certainly the marks of some battle, some life unimaginably more difficult than my own; I ask him to tell me what had happened to his hand. And he says:

I was with the Mujahideen, and the Russians did this. I was with the Mujahideen, and an enemy faction of Mujahideen did this. I was with the Russians, I was known to have assisted the Russians, I did informer's work for Babrak Karmal, my name is in the files if they haven't been destroyed, the names I gave are in the files, there are no more files, I stole bread for my starving family, I stole bread *from* a starving family, I profaned, betrayed, according to some stricture I erred and they chopped off the fingers of my hand. *Look, look at my country, look at my Kabul, my city, what is left of my city? The streets are as bare as the mountains now, the buildings are as ragged as mountains and as bare and empty of life, there is no life here only fear, we do not live in the buildings now, we live in terror in the cellars in the caves in the mountains, only God can save us now, only order can save us now, only God's Law harsh and strictly administered can save us now, only The Department for the Promotion of Virtue and the Prevention of Vice can save us now, only terror can save us from ruin, only neverending war, save us from terror and neverending war, save my wife they are stoning my wife, they are chasing her with sticks, save my wife save my daughter from punishment by God, save us from God, from war, from exile, from oil exploration, from no oil exploration, from the West, from the children with rifles, carrying stones, only children with rifles, carrying stones, can save us now.* You will never understand. It is hard, it was hard work to get into the U.K. I am happy here in the U.K. I am terrified I will be made to leave the U.K. I cannot wait to leave the U.K. I despise the U.K. I voted for John Major. I voted for Tony Blair. I did not, I cannot vote, I do not believe in voting, the people who ruined my hand were right to do so, they were wrong to do so, my hand is most certainly ruined, *you will never understand,* why are you buying so many hats?

(Little pause)

We all romp about, grieving, wondering, but with rare exception we mostly remain suspended in the Rhetorical Colloidal Forever that agglutinates between Might and Do. "Might do, might do." I have a friend who says that. "Off to the cinema, care to come?" "Might do." "Would you eat a potato plucked from that soil?" "Might do." Jesus wants you hot or cold but she will hedge her every bet, and why should she not? What has this century taught the civilized if not contempt for those who merely contemplate; the lockup and the lethal injection for those who Do. Awful times, as I have said, our individual degrees of culpability for said awfulness being entirely bound-up in our correspondent degrees of action, malevolent or not, or in our correspondent degrees of inertia, which can be taken as a form of malevolent action if you've a mind to see it that way. I do. I've such a mind. My husband . . . Never mind. We shall most of us be adjudged guilty when we are summoned before the Judgment Seat. But guilt? Personal guilt? *(Wringing hands)* Oh, oh . . . No more morally useful or impressive than adult nappy rash, and nearly as unsightly, and ought to be kept as private, ought guilt, as any other useless unimpressive unsightly inflammation. Not suitable for public exchange. And all conversation such as we are having, and though you've said nothing whatsoever we are still conversing, I think, since what I say is driven by fear of you, sitting there before me, by absolute terror of your censure and disdain, and so you need say nothing, you would only weaken your position, whatever it may be, whatever you may be making of this, by speaking, I mean, look at me, look at what I am doing, to myself, to what you must think of me, if ever you chance upon me on _____ *(Gesture)*, out shopping, what will you think? Avoid! Her! All conversation constitutes public exchange was my point, and there are rules of engagement, and skin rash should be displayed in public only for medicinal restorative purposes, inviting the healing rays of the sun and the drying authority of the fresh crisp breeze, and not for the garnering of admiration and the harvesting of sympathy. For most of us deserve neither, and I include myself in that harsh judgment, no matter how guilty we are or feel ourselves to be, my optimism notwithstanding.

I watch as he puts the ten hats in a carrier-bag and feel no surprise when he informs someone in the back of the shop, in Pushto, in which language as I mentioned I now find myself fluent, he's taking the rest of the afternoon off, and he offers me his right hand. I take it and we go out of the shop but no longer on _____ *(Gesture)*, we are standing on a road, a road in Kabul. I hold on tight to his ruined right hand, and he leads me on a guided tour through his city. There are the mountains, unreal as clouds; it is shamelessly sweet, the wreckage rack and ruination all there of course, it's ineffaceable now, this holocaustal effacement, but the gardens of Babur Shah are there too, just like the outdated guidebook promises, and the room in which handsome Shah Shujah, about thirty years of age, of olive complexion and thick black beard, puppet monarch of the British Mission, detested and soon to be murdered by his own insurgent people, displays himself to breathtaking effect, his visitors imagining him at first to be

dressed in an armor of jewels, how impractical *that* would be, but actually he wears a green tunic over which are worked flowers of gold and a breast plate of diamonds, shaped like flattened fleurs-de-lis, ornaments of the same kind on each thigh, emeralds above the elbows, diamonds on each wrist, strings of pearls like cross belts but loose, a crown not encrusted with jewels but apparently entirely formed of those precious materials, the whole so complicated and dazzling it is difficult to understand and impossible to describe, and the throne is covered with a cloth adorned with pearls . . .
(She cries softly)
And the scent of the hat merchant takes me by surprise, toasted almonds, and he smiles a broader shy smile which shatters his face into a thousand shards and near a place called Bemaru, thought to be the grave of Bibi Mahru, the Moon-Faced Lady, who died of grief when her betrothed was reported slain on the battlefield, but he wasn't slain, he'd only lost his hand, near her grave, visited by mothers with ailing children, even today, *especially today* when there are many many such cases, many ailing children—demurely hidden from the sight of the ailing and the destitute and war-ravaged we, the hat merchant and I, make love beneath a chinar tree, which is it is my guess a kind of plane tree, beloved of the Moghuls. We kiss, his breath is very bitter, he places his hand inside me, it seems to me his whole hand inside me, and it seems to me a whole hand. And there are flocks of pigeons the nearby villagers keep banded with bronze rings about their legs, and they are released each afternoon for flight, and there is frequently, in the warmer months, kite flying to be seen on the heights of Bemaru.
(Pause)
I sign the receipt, I have paid, he hands me the carrier-bag stuffed with my purchase and with his smile indicates we are done and I should depart. And a chill wind blows up my bones and I long to be back in the safety of my kitchen and I leave the shop pondering the possibility that my prescribed

dosage of . . . Mealy-aza-opzamene is too strong, or that sampling my husband's pills . . . perhaps these two chemicals are immiscible.

And yes in fact I do have children, well, *one*. A child. For whom alas nothing ever seems to go well. The older she gets. My fault entirely I'm sure or at least so I am told by my husband the near-mute purveyor of reproachful lids-lowered glances. But this is neither here nor there. We all loved one another, once, but today it simply isn't so or isn't what it used to be, it's . . . well, love.

I love the world. I know how that sounds, inexcusable and vague, but it's all I can say for myself, I love the world, really I do . . . *Love.* Not the vast and unembraceable and orbicular world, this is no gigantic rhapsodic—for all that one might suspect a person who uses words like gigantine—God!—of narcissism, my love is not that overstretched self-aggrandizing hyperinflated sort of adulation which seeks in the outsized and the impossible-to-clearly-comprehend a reflection commensurate with its own oceanic . . . of, well, I suppose of the extent to which the soul excuse me I mean the self is always an insoluble mystery to the narcissist who flatters herself that feeling of vagueness always hanging about her which not a salt in the world can cure is something grand, oceanic, titanically erotic while of course what it really is is nothing more than an inadequately shaped unsteady incoherent . . . quoggy sort of bubble where the solid core ought to be.

I love . . . this guidebook. Its foxed unfingered pages. Forgotten words: "Quizilbash." Its sorrowing supercessional displacement by all that has since occurred. So lost; and also so familiar. The home *(She makes the gesture)* away from home. *Recognizable*: not how vast but how *crowded* the world is, consequences to *everything*: the Macedonians, marching east; one tribe displacing another; or one moment in which the heart strays from itself and love is . . . gone? What after all is a child but the history of all that has befallen her, a succession of displacements, bloody, beautiful? How could any mother not love the world? What else is love but recognition? Love's nothing to do with happiness. Power has to do with happiness. Love has only to do with home.

(Little pause)

Where stands the homebody, safe in her kitchen, on her culpable shore, suffering uselessly watching others perishing in the sea, wringing her plump little maternal hands, oh, oh. Never *joining* the drowning. Her feet, neither rooted nor moving. The ocean is deep and cold and erasing. But how dreadful, really unpardonable, to remain dry.

Look at her, look at her, she is so unforgivably dry. Neither here nor there. She does not drown, she . . . succumbs. To Luxury. She sinks. Terror-struck, down, down into . . . um, the dangerous silent spaces, or rather places, with gravity and ground, down into the terrible silent gardens of the private, in the frightening echoing silence of which a grieving voice might be heard, chattering away, keening, rocking, shrouded, trying to express that which she lacks all power to express but which she knows must be expressed or else . . . death. And she would sound I suppose rather like what I sound like now:

(Whispers:)

Avoid! Her!

And now my daughter, come home as one does. Mother knows mysteries; hence her implacable scrabbling at my gate. I so wanted her to be out in the world, my daughter. Of use. But she must have and may not budge, and I understand, I am her mother, she is . . . starving. I . . . withhold my touch. The touch which does not understand is the touch which corrupts, the touch which does not understand that which it touches is the touch which corrupts that which it touches, and which corrupts itself.

And so yes, when unexpectedly a curtain I'd not noticed before is parted by a ruined hand, which then beckons: there is a country so at the heart of the world the world has forgotten it, where one might seek in submission the unanswered need. And I find myself improbably considering . . .

(Pause)
The hats at the party are a brilliant success. My guests adore them. They are hard to keep on the head, made for smaller people than the people we are and so they slip off, which generates amusement, and the guests exchange them while dancing, kaleidoscopic and self-effacing and I think perhaps to our surprise in some small way meltingly intimate, someone else's hat atop your head, making your scalp stiffen at the imagined strangeness; and to a select group in the kitchen I tell about the merchant who sold them to me, and a friend wisely asks, how do you even know he's Afghan, and of course that's a good question, and the fact is I don't. And I wonder for an instant that I didn't ask. "Would you make love to a stranger with a mutilated hand if the opportunity was offered you?" "Might do," she says. Frank Sinatra is playing: such an awful awful man, such perfect perfect music! A paradox!
(Frank Sinatra starts to sing "It's Nice to Go Trav'ling." She sings the first two verses with him, putting the hats back in the shopping bag, one by one:)

> It's very nice to go trav'ling
> To Paris, London and Rome
> It's oh so nice to go trav'ling,
> But it's so much nicer yes it's so much nicer
> To come home.
> It's very nice to just wander
> The camel route to Iraq,
> It's oh so nice to just wander
> But it's so much nicer yes it's oh so nice
> To wander back . . .

(The music fades. The Homebody stands, takes the coat draped over the back of the empty chair, and puts it on. Buttoning the coat, she says:)
In the seventeenth century the Persian poet Sa'ib-I-Tabrizi was summoned to the court of the Moghul emperors in Agra,

and on his way he passed, as one does, Kabul, the city in the Hindu Kush, and he wrote a poem, for he had been touched by its strangeness and beauty, moved only as one may be moved through an encounter with the beautiful and strange; and he declared he would never be the same again:

(She picks up the guidebook, but does not open it)

> Oh the beautiful city of Kabul wears a rugged mountain
> skirt,
> And the rose is jealous of its lash-like thorns.
> The dust of Kabul's blowing soil smarts lightly in my
> eyes,
> But I love her, for knowledge and love both come from
> her dust.
> I sing bright praises to her colorful tulips,
> The beauty of her trees makes me blush.
> Every street in Kabul fascinates the eye.
> In the bazaars, Egypt's caravans pass by.
> No one can count the beauteous moons on her rooftops,
> And hundreds of lovely suns hide behind her walls.
> Her morning laugh is as gay as flowers,
> Her dark nights shine like beautiful hair.
> Her tuneful nightingales sing with flame in their throats,
> Their fiery songs fall like burning leaves.
> I sing to the gardens of Kabul;
> Even Paradise is jealous of their greenery.

SCENE 2

A hotel room in Kabul, luxurious by Kabuli standards. Two single beds. Milton Ceiling is seated on one bed, Mullah Aftar Ali Durranni is seated on the other. Doctor Qari Shah is standing beside and slightly behind Mullah Durranni; Quango Twistleton is standing behind Milton.
Priscilla Ceiling is seated in a chair behind a bedsheet which has been hung across one corner of the room. There's a lamp on a small table behind her; her shadow is cast on the bedsheet.
It's early morning. The mood in the room is very grim.
Doctor Qari Shah is speaking, brisk, professional, kind, occasionally consulting a notebook.

DOCTOR QARI SHAH
The left clavicle was traumatically separated from the conacoid process, also the infra spinous fossa quite, ah, shattered by a heavy blow, most probably as the woman was dragged—your wife—by her upper limb, arm that is to say, up and down rubble-strewn streets over piles of bomb debris. After dislocation of the humerus from the glenohumeral joint, there was separation and consequent calamitous exsanguination from the humeral stump. Perhaps occurring as the wife attempts self-defense. *(He holds his left hand in front of his face as if warding off a blow)* The, ah, right gynglymus and enarthrodial joints are found to have been twisted to nonanatomical ninety-degree positions and the arm . . . separated by dull force. The right side of the os innominatum is

also crushed. She is being beaten repeatedly with stakes and rusted iron rebar rods, remember. From the surmisable positions of the assailants and so forth, we believe there were ten persons implicit, approximately so.
My English. I have study medicine in Edinburgh, but long ago. I apologize.
(He pauses. No one moves or says anything. He resumes:)
The axillary fascia of the right, ah, hemispherical eminence, um, mamma, um, *breast*, torn off either by force of a blow or as the corpus is dragged. Her left eye having been enucleated, and from dull force the occiput *(He indicates the back of the skull)* sheared cleanly off. And consequently to which, spillage of, ah, contents.
It may be ventured there seems to have been no forcible invasion of the introitus. She was not dishonored. Your wife.

MULLAH AFTAR ALI DURRANNI
Tear up. *(He pronounces "Tear" like "teardrop")*

MILTON
I'm afraid I . . . ?

MULLAH AFTAR ALI DURRANNI
Tear up. She—
(He points to a copy of the International Herald Tribune *on the bed near Milton)* You are reading this?

MILTON
It's two days old. I bought it in the Islamabad air terminal.

MULLAH AFTAR ALI DURRANNI
I may take it please?

(Milton nods. Mullah Durranni takes the Tribune *and rips it to small pieces.*
Little pause, everyone looks at the paper scraps.)

MILTON

Oh. *Torn* up.

MULLAH AFTAR ALI DURRANNI

Yes just so. The lady, she have been torn apart to pieces.

(Silence.)

QUANGO

Bloody, bloody hell.

MULLAH AFTAR ALI DURRANNI

She have wandered through Cheshme Khedre, where undetonated land mines are. She wander alone by the . . . Way ran nee-hah? *(To Doctor Qari Shah)* How it's said?

DOCTOR QARI SHAH

Ruins.

MULLAH AFTAR ALI DURRANNI

Yes, *ruins* by Cheshme Khedre, where nobody live there any longer, why she was there? In these bad times, why this lady your wife come to Kabul? She have been informed upon to have been not clad in decent attire for street, not wearing burqa, uncovered. Attack such as this, have never happen before in Kabul, never in Afghanistan.

Since last week President Clinton have bombed the people in Khost, many killed, the people are very angry against Western aggression-disregard-disrespect for Afghanistan. And also she have been carrying openly this thing:

(From a paper sack he removes a yellow discman, headphones attached, and he hands it to Milton. Milton opens the lid of the discman, looks at the CD inside, closes it.)

MULLAH AFTAR ALI DURRANNI

Impious music which is an affront to Islam, to dress like so and then the music, these are regrettable.

PRISCILLA

(From behind the bedsheet) What is it? May I see?

(Milton steps behind the bedsheet and hands the discman to Priscilla. She holds it, then puts on the headphones and pushes the play button. All this is in lamplit silhouette against the bedsheet. Milton returns, sits on the bed.)

MILTON

It's, ah, Frank Sinatra. "Come Fly with Me."

MULLAH AFTAR ALI DURRANNI

We search for the criminals who have done this thing, and when they are seized they shall be put to death. Rough boys, criminals, and also perhaps they believe incorrectly she is American.

QUANGO

They've come to claim her body, Minister Durranni.

MULLAH AFTAR ALI DURRANNI

This we cannot know. Where it is.

(Little pause.)

QUANGO

You lost her body?

MULLAH AFTAR ALI DURRANNI

In Cheshme Khedre where these rough boys kill her there is nearby the UNESCO hospital but this is closed. So she is taken to the Ladies Hospital though already she is dead. Here

Doctor Qari Shah inspected her remains. For some cause, she is then transported to Ibn Sena—you say "Avicenna"—Hospital on Sipah Salar Muhhamad Nadir Kahn Wat. In Ladies Hospital there are almost no suture, antibiotics, medicines of this sort; but as she is dead, this lady, that ought not to have been considered. Also as well at Abdullah Ibn Sena there is no medicine, anywhere, anywhere in Afghanistan. But this morning hearing you have arrived from Peshawar, coming to call for the dead lady at Ibn Sena, she is found not to be there. Information regrettably is scarce. We are searching now for where she is. You shall stay here. Or return home.

QUANGO
May I ask. With respect. *(In Dari)* Baw tamawmay eht'rawm. Chirah bahroyaheen haw zarooree-bood kehgosh baydehand . . . um . . . *(With respect. Why . . . was it necessary for these people to listen to this . . .)* impenetrable litany of medical horrors? To frighten them?

(Ignoring this, Mullah Durranni stands. He turns to Milton.)

MULLAH AFTAR ALI DURRANNI
To you and your daughter, every Afghan heart laments for the mother. Death we know. Kabul is not a city for Western tourist women, we do not want them. In sha' Allah. No thing may be made or unmade unless Allah wills it. He fills our hearts with griefs, to see if we shall be strong. You are kaafer, you do not understand, but this is Allah's way.

(Little pause.)

MILTON
Yes, yes . . . I see. Thank you.

DOCTOR QARI SHAH
I have studied medicine in Edinburgh. I apologize if my English is . . . impenetrable. *(To Milton)* I am truly sorry.

MILTON

No, it's . . . quite good.

MULLAH AFTAR ALI DURRANNI

These also were hers.
(He reaches in the sack and removes three hats, rough wool berets, not like the ones in Scene 1, and a book) Several fine pacooli. Perhaps gifts for you, her husband.

(Mullah Durranni hands the book to Doctor Qari Shah, who reads the cover:)

DOCTOR QARI SHAH

An Historical Guide to the City of Kabul.

MULLAH AFTAR ALI DURRANNI

But in Kabul now there is no history. There is only God. This is no more a city for . . . *(To Doctor Qari Shah)* Kattel ow tama sha kawol?

DOCTOR QARI SHAH

Sightseeing.

MULLAH AFTAR ALI DURRANNI

Precisely. No.

(Mullah Durranni stands, nods to Milton, who nods back, vaguely; Mullah Durranni leaves.
Doctor Qari Shah gives Milton a sudden, fierce embrace before following Mullah Durranni out.
Quango lingers. Priscilla pulls the bedsheet down and stays seated, holding the sheet in one hand, the discman in the other.
Milton looks at Quango, speechless.)

QUANGO

You'll want to be left alone now.

I should like to help. I shall make inquiries about . . . The
body. And I'll . . . call again, if I might, or . . .

(Priscilla lights a cigarette.
Quango leaves.)

PRISCILLA

He works for the *British* government? Doesn't seem . . . gov-
ernmental, what was his name?

MILTON

Twistleton? Bingo? Pongo? Pongo Twistleton?

(He starts to giggle. She starts to giggle.)

MILTON

Can that be?

PRISCILLA

Pongo Twistleton is a character in a P. G. Wodehouse novel,
Dad.

MILTON

In some semi-official capacity, apparently. There's no embassy,
so . . . *(He bursts into tears)*

PRISCILLA

I've never seen you cry before.

MILTON

Yes, well, this is what it looks like.

(He continues to cry, cradling his shoe.
She sits. She looks at the discman. Silence for a bit, then:)

PRISCILLA

(*Holding out the discman*) You'd think a thing like this would be of some value, wouldn't you, on the black market? They'd have nicked it, her assailants, it's what I'd have done if I'd no money.

MILTON

Music. It's . . . contra Islam.

PRISCILLA

And these were very *pious* boys who beat her to death, do you think?

MILTON

I'd kill for a drink.

PRISCILLA

Drinks are illegal here.
All those rusted iron rebar rods, flailing away, and it hasn't a scratch.

MILTON

Japanese plastics, durable stuff.

PRISCILLA

Thus spake the electronics engineer.

MILTON

It's all ultimately explained by high-impact polystyrenes.

PRISCILLA

Do you think she screamed?
She must have been . . . terrified, and in terrible pain.

MILTON

They say in some circumstances the screams simply come out of you and you don't know immediately who it is doing the screaming, you have not made the decision to scream and yet screams are issuing forth. Which is probably a good thing, because it implies that within you there is a person more competent than yourself at assessing and responding to danger.

(Little pause.)

PRISCILLA

Something's wrong.

MILTON

Everything is wrong, Priss, but—

PRISCILLA

Maybe she's kidnapped. Maybe she's hurt, in a hospital, and they're hiding her for some reason. We should try to call the hospitals and—
(She picks up the phone, jiggles the cradle buttons to get a dial tone)
Dead.
And that mullah? Were you impressed with the beard and the turban? I wasn't impressed. He ripped up that paper to scare us.

MILTON

People remain at home when tragedies happen and the government arranges things like shipping bodies.

PRISCILLA

The government! The government couldn't tell us if she was alive or dead.
We still don't *know*.

MILTON

Don't know . . . ?
What?

PRISCILLA

We don't know she's dead.

You haven't asked a single question since we woke up and found she'd left. She pops off to Kabul and you, it's like you expected all this.

MILTON

She *warned us*, she said she was considering this, this—

PRISCILLA

(Overlapping) It was ludicrous, all that.

MILTON

(Overlapping) well what would one call it? Holiday?

PRISCILLA

(Overlapping) "Os innominatum"?

MILTON

(Overlapping) We simply couldn't credit it.

PRISCILLA

(Overlapping) What's that? The, the . . . *nameless bone*? What the fuck is *that*?

MILTON

(Overlapping) Well she could be so preposterous, so yes in a sense I always *expected* her to do something, something disagreeable, and—

PRISCILLA

(Overlapping) And all right, you screamed at her and I shot her a basilisk stare or two but was that a reason to pack? To *go to Afghanistan*? And five days later she's dead, it's like a dream, it's . . .

Maybe she's hiding. From us.

MILTON

SHE IS DEAD! *Reuters* has reported it!

PRISCILLA

I'm going out for a bit.

MILTON

Out . . . SIDE?! The hell you are.

(She picks up the discman, and the guidebook, and starts for the door.)

MILTON

It's *extremely dangerous* out there. Am I to take two bodies home?

PRISCILLA

Better than none.

MILTON

And think, Priscilla, what she must, um, *look* like. You can't want to see that.

PRISCILLA

I don't know, Milton. I might.

(She goes to a parcel on the bed, wrapped in newsprint and tied with string. She opens it. She removes a green burqa. She picks up the burqa, examining it. She puts it over her head, not sure how to, wrestling with it till it slips into place. Looking around, through the face-grille, she laughs. Then:)

PRISCILLA

It's as if I've contracted an exotic ophthalmological condition. *(She starts to leave. She stops)*

MILTON

What? What is—

PRISCILLA

I'm scared obviously.
And if they have ripped her open at least I'll finally get to see
her fucking secrets.

(She exits the room, slamming the door.
Milton goes to the door, puts his hand on the knob, then
removes it. He stands shouting through the door, but not open-
ing it:)

MILTON

Priscilla! Come back!
(He sits heavily on the bed) Jesus Christ.
I am unmarried.

SCENE 3

On a street in Kabul.
Priscilla is in her burqa, trying to read the guidebook's small map through the burqa's grille, holding it close, changing angles so as to find the strongest light.
A group of women pass by, all shrouded head to toe in burqas, whispering.

PRISCILLA
Um, hullo, can you tell me where the Ladies Hospital is. Or the Red Crescent offices, or the U.N. compound, it's all turned around somehow. I can't read any of the signs. Do you speak English?

LADY IN BURQA
(In Dari) Mah nah may donam cheezayk'shomaw may go ayd. Bah cheezabon shomaw harf mayzanayd? *(I do not under-stand what you are saying. What language are you speaking?)*

PRISCILLA
My mother was . . . They say she was murdered.

LADY IN BURQA
Mother?

(Priscilla tosses off her burqa. She's wearing the discman on a belt around her waist, the headphones in her ears.)

PRISCILLA

Yes! And I am lost. Is this building the—

(The women react with consternation when she throws off her burqa. They hurry off.
Priscilla picks up the guidebook, sits on the curb, lights a ciga-rette, starts to peruse the map.
Immediately a bearded man in green shalwah kamiz appears, wearing a black turban, carrying a Kalashnikov and a rubber hose.
He watches Priscilla, who is not aware of his presence. A moment, then he advances on her, brandishing the hose, frightening her—although his tone is more bemused and curious than vicious.)

THE MUNKRAT

(In Pashtun) Zan putka, ow segret-day watchawa. Mukh-kay lahagha cheh woo dey wah hoom. T'yow wah beysharmah khazah yay. T'pah hay zhey cheh dah ayjahzah neshtah. Watchawah os. *(Cover yourself and put out that cigarette before I whip you, you shameless idiot. Put it out now.)*

(Priscilla, terrified, in a panic, leaps to her feet, dropping the book, throwing the burqa back on, all tangled, the cigarette still in her mouth. She drops the cigarette once inside the burqa and frantically shakes the fabric out, then scrambles to retrieve the book, all the while apologizing.)

PRISCILLA

(Overlapping with the Munkrat) Wait, wait please, I'm sorry, I just . . . keep spilling things and I . . . Wait, wait, stop, I don't speak, I speak English I . . . I am English, British, oh I've dropped my fucking book and . . . Oh fuck I've dropped the lit cigarette, I'll set it on fire, oh my God.

(She throws the burqa off and shakes it out.)

THE MUNKRAT

(Overlapping with above) Sta millah sokh day? Pah kum zai-ikay oseezhee? Dumrah baday woowahum cheh la gar zay dohnah patah shay! Aya t'koom fahishah khazah-yay? *(Who is your husband? Where do you live? I am going to beat you till you can't walk, are you some kind of harlot?)*

(During the preceding tirade, Khwaja Aziz Mondanabosh enters, watches, then approaches the Munkrat with deference.)

KHWAJA

Meheraboni woklah da gharbi khezah prayzdah. Da zima mass ul yut-day. Z'da hagha maharam-yum. Da injalai zima ur-ra-radah. Da injalai pah charahee Pashtunistan Hotel kay noom-eh sapt k'laydah. Ow hagha-may delta plartahyay rahoowustaydah. *(Please forgive this Western lady. She is my responsibility, I am her mahram, she is my niece, she is a registered guest staying at the Pashtunistan Square Hotel, I am bringing her to her father.)*

THE MUNKRAT

Da khazah wallay yawazay gurzee? Da bil kul yawah fahishah ow lawanda khazah dah. *(Why is she wandering alone then? She's lost, she was exposing herself.)*

KHWAJA

T'khawmakhah munzh dwarlo wobakhah. Da khazah dayr wooraydilay dah ow munzh p'marg-kay sharmay dilay yoo. *(You must forgive us both, sir, she is terror-stricken, and we are both mortally embarrassed.)*

THE MUNKRAT

Ka ko, t'Amreeka yah yeh? *(What, she's American?)*

KHWAJA

Nah, khazah Inglees-sah dah. *(English.)*

THE MUNKRAT

T'pahayzhay cheh zeh bah tahsoh dwarloh woo wah hoom. *(I could beat you both, you know.)*

KHWAJA

Zeh wa'adakawoom cheh dah khazah— *(I will make sure she—)*

THE MUNKRAT

Zeh fekehr kahwoom cheh dah khuzah lezh kootee woo wah hal shee sirf doomrah-cheh haghatah sargandashee . . . *(I think I will, she should be beaten a little, just to make sure she . . .)*
(To Khwaja) T'yahwah khwah tah shah. *(Move aside, you.)*
(To Priscilla, brandishing the rubber hose) Dah day Islami shari'yat mukhaulef kar-day— *(It is forbidden by the laws of the Islamic—)*

(Khwaja snatches the hose from the Munkrat's upraised hand. The Munkrat immediately wales on Khwaja, who kneels down, supplicant. The Munkrat, while yelling at Khwaja, kicks him, knocking him onto his back.)

THE MUNKRAT

T'doomrah joorat kaway cheh z'mah door-r-r-rah neesay khugah! Lass dooray dah khazah tah— *(How dare you grab my whip, you pig! Ten lashes for her and—)*

KHWAJA

(Calm but stern) Dah bah ghalatah kar wee cheh dah khuzah woo wah hal shee. Hagha yawah milmana dah ow dah kho de mil mastiyah deh oosool puhrkhelahv yawah kar-wee— *(It would be wrong to beat her, she is a guest, our guest, it would be offensive to the laws of hospitality to—)*

(Little pause. The Munkrat holds out his hand. Khwaja hands him the hose.)

THE MUNKRAT
(To Khwaja) Dah khazah bertah hotel tah bozah. Ow zeh nah gharloom cheh tasoh dwarloh b'ya pah sark-kay woo wee noom. *(Take her back to the hotel, don't let me find either of you on the street again today.)*

KHWAJA
Khodaw hafez. *(May God be with you always.)*

(The Munkrat brandishes the hose as if preparing to strike Khwaja, just to frighten him. Then he leaves.)

KHWAJA
(To Priscilla, in Esperanto) Ĉu vi parolas Esperanto? *(Do you speak Esperanto?)*

PRISCILLA
What?

KHWAJA
Esperanto?

PRISCILLA
I . . . What?

KHWAJA
(Pleasant but urgent, nervous) That a lady should be unescorted, without family, not permissible, but I will be your uncle! If by your aimless wanderings and the guidebook I am right in concluding that you wish to see Kabul?

PRISCILLA
Just let me . . . Wait.

(She bends over, breathes deeply. Khwaja looks over his shoulder, nervous.)

KHWAJA

My name is Khwaja Aziz Mondanabosh. You are the distressed lady whose mother was murdered.

PRISCILLA

Oh.

KHWAJA

I am a mahram, the best the city has to offer, I have contemplated upon its every brick, and even better: I am a poet! All Tajiks, we are all poets, but some are not so good, really, they try but I am actually a good poet, quite competent in Dari and even better in Esperanto.

PRISCILLA

Are you Taliban?

KHWAJA

No, Tajik. As I said.

(She doesn't understand.)

KHWAJA

The Taliban prefer Tajiks far away, in Tajikistan. The Taliban are mostly Pashtun and Afghan Tajiks are mostly out of work.

PRISCILLA

You know the city?

KHWAJA

Since 1993 I am a Kabuli. Before that, Earl's Court, ducky. And before that, Kabul, where I was born. Am I to be your uncle or ought I to push off?

(Little pause.)

PRISCILLA

Five pounds for the day.

KHWAJA

As you wish.

PRISCILLA

Ten pounds?

KHWAJA

I will be the cheapest family you ever had.

PRISCILLA

How did you know about my mother?

KHWAJA

It is a gossipy city, Kabul. Full of widows.

PRISCILLA

They said she was torn to pieces. Something about her . . . occiput.

KHWAJA

I shall take you to the morgue at the College of Medicine. The college is closed of course but not the morgue.

PRISCILLA

If she was only injured, they'd have her in hospital.

KHWAJA

Is she not dead?

PRISCILLA

I don't know.

KHWAJA

I will take you to the hospitals, then, where sepsis is pervasive. It would be wise to replace the burqa.

(She puts on the burqa.)

PRISCILLA

I'm . . . You're to be my uncle?

(Little pause. He looks at her.)

KHWAJA

Five years ago in the fighting just three blocks away, a mortar shell and good-bye dear gentle brother, estimable sister-in-law, nephews, beloved niece.

PRISCILLA

Is that true?

(Khwaja bows a little, neither affirming nor denying.)

KHWAJA

But see, she has returned to heartsick old Khwaja, as all my dreams foretold.

SCENE 4

Meanwhile, back at the hotel:
Milton and Quango in the hotel room, sitting on the beds.
Quango has a bottle of scotch and they are drinking. Milton
has put on one of the pacoolis.

QUANGO
One of six newborn babies die here. One in every six. About
half the remaining Afghan children die before they reach the
age of five. And thirty-five percent of those hardy survivors
are drastically malnourished, I mean little potbellied skele-
tons, starving slowly to death. On the Human Index Rank
this place is 169th of 174 countries, it's not really a state at
all, it's a populated disaster. The only reason it's not considered *the* worst for women is because the Afghans don't do
genital mutilation. Most of the arable land is land-mined.

MILTON
Why on earth are you here?

QUANGO
I love this place.
This used to be a fully functioning country, you see? With,
ah, secretaries in modest dresses and . . . and lady ticket-
takers at the cinema. And with cinemas, so they tell me. And
standing buildings. And roads. Only twenty years ago.
It drives a man to drink, Milton. If I may call you Milton.

MILTON

You may, Mr. Twistleton, if you top me up.

QUANGO

(Doing so) Quango.

MILTON

My daughter informs me that Quango Twistleton is a character in a novel by . . . someone.

QUANGO

Wodehouse, but that would be *Pongo* Twistleton.

MILTON

And you are *Quango*.

QUANGO

I am actually Dave, but . . . it's a rather stupid story, I worked for a NGO, a nongovernmental organization, which, because it performed infrequent services for Her Majesty's foreign secretary, was deemed a *quasi*-NGO by my disdainful purist comrades in the field of human aid. Quasi-NGO, hence, Quango, and since my surname is actually Twistleton, absurd as that may seem, well there you are.

MILTON

Is it a good novel?

QUANGO

Mr. Wodehouse wrote only good novels. Or rather he wrote the same good novel over and over. Pongo is the hapless hero of several, the most sublime of which being *Uncle Fred in the Springtime.*

(Milton holds up his empty glass.)

MILTON

It's a crime, my daughter informs me. Drinking.

QUANGO

It is.

MILTON

(Holds the glass toward Quango) Make me a criminal.

(Quango pours.)

QUANGO

For the commission of which crime one can jolly well find
oneself Toyota-trucked out to the old soccer stadium and . . .
(He makes a gesture indicating a hand being chopped off)
Rough boys, these Taliban. Growing up in a refugee camp, it
coarsens the sensibilities. They have a reading of Islam un-
like . . . any other in the world.
I stay because Afghanistan broke my heart.
I'm an embarrassing sort of person.

MILTON

My daughter broke mine.

QUANGO

She did, did she?

MILTON

Sorrow causes damage. You shed vitality all along the way.

QUANGO

She's quite lovely.

MILTON

She is?

QUANGO

Your daughter.

MILTON

I know who you mean.

QUANGO

Blew my mind.
That's better. Afghanistan blew my mind, Milton, to bits, and now I cannot get it back.
It's like a disease, this place.

SCENE 5

Several hours later, same day, evening is approaching. Khwaja is leading Priscilla, clad in her burqa, up a steep rocky path to the top of a hill.

KHWAJA
Several hundred British soldiers were slaughtered here in 1841. This pillar marks the—

PRISCILLA
We already passed the pillar for the . . . the soldiers, hours and hours ago. Are we going in circles?

KHWAJA
There are many pillars, many slaughtered British soldiers.

(She tears the burqa off. She looks at the landscape.)

PRISCILLA
Oh, *beautiful*.

KHWAJA
Isn't it?
That is Bemaru, over there. That was the dome of Ziarat-I-Jan Baz, now destroyed, and that is Ziarat Panjeshah, what's left of it, and those white stones in the walls of the cliff . . .

(He points to a place in the distance. They have to squint to see.)

KHWAJA

Those are the bones of a dragon. Hazrat Ali, the fourth caliph, son-in-law of the Prophet, visited Kabul and slew the dragon. I have composed a poem on the battle, unfortunately it is in Esperanto.

PRISCILLA

Oh, *yes*, yes, that *is* unfortunate.
I detest poetry.
(She lights a cigarette)
Oh my God it's so good to, to stop, to draw breath. I haven't breathed since . . . Well for days.
Oh my God I've never seen anything so . . . I've never traveled. Not anywhere. We went to Paris once, but I didn't look. Who'd have thought Hiroshima after the bomb would look so lovely?
There isn't enough good will in the world to rebuild it. What a godawful place to die.

KHWAJA

As what place is not?
There's little daylight left.

PRISCILLA

Should we try once more at the, the Ladies Hospital? I'll try not to vomit.

KHWAJA

I would like to entrust you with something.

(He takes a sheaf of papers tied with string from an inner pocket and offers them to Priscilla.)

KHWAJA

Here is a sheaf of my poems.

(She does not take them.)

KHWAJA

These are not for you, who neither speak nor read Esperanto and who also despises poetry. When you will return to London, might you agree to deliver them? To a fellow Tajik, an Esperantist, Mr. Sahar lives at 17 Pindock Mews, Maida Vale, from Waterloo Station you take the tube to—

PRISCILLA

I know how to get to Maida Vale.

(Again he holds out the poems. Again she doesn't take them.)

KHWAJA

When I was your age, already I had a good wife and a sweet little girl. I sold vacuum cleaner parts and I was a socialist. A poet must be a thinking man, so I was a socialist, as thinking men often were in those days. But not a communist, no, for what is the world without Allah in it? Fitna, disorder, misery, madness. But I fought with the communists, and Zahir Shah went out, and all the reforms commenced, women literacy campaigns, elimination of the veil, too much too fast. One thing and then another and I went to prison.

PRISCILLA

You were in prison?

KHWAJA

Pole-I-Charki, it's called.
My sweet wife and child went to London, she had family there, the ICRC helped.
I was in prison for six wretched years.

PRISCILLA

My God.

KHWAJA

I missed the uprisings, the Soviet invasions—Babrak Karmal was a communist, but when the Soviets put him in he doesn't let me out, why, who can say? It was an appalling time. Doctor Najibullah replaced Babrak Karmal and let some of us out. He cared for the people, Najibullah. He was KHAD, secret police, and he tortured, they say. He was Pashtun, but still not a bad old bastard.

I wanted to learn English while I was in prison, for after, for when I was released, I could join my family in London. And my cellmate—a very old man, he had been in prison for forty years!—he spoke fluent English, several other languages as well—a real product of the cosmopolitan days of old King Amanullah Kahn. I asked him, please, to teach me English. He refused; he would teach me something much better: an international language, spoken in every nation on earth. I had never heard of such a marvel! Esperanto. It was created by a Polish Jew, Zamenhof, who believed that until we could speak to one another in a mother tongue which draws from us our common humanity, peace will never be attained. Who doesn't want peace? Who would not want to be able to speak the world's language? He was a good teacher, my cellmate, a good, patient man, I dream of him from time to time.

He was, unfortunately, mistaken about one important thing. I arrived in London speaking better Esperanto than my teacher. No one could understand me.

I had written three hundred poems in prison, all in Esperanto. I find that I have an ear for its particular staccato music, with its regular system of affixes attached to simple roots, connoting verb, place, opposition . . . I love its modern hyperrational ungainliness. To me it sounds not universally at home, rather homeless, stateless, a global refugee patois.

PRISCILLA

I don't know what it sounds like.

KHWAJA

Sidante en la ĝardeno, mi aŭdis bruon.
Vidante sin en la ĝardeno, mi vokis al si.
Vokite, si tuj venis.
La tera estis tute kovrita per neĝo.
Sidante, atendante, mi aŭdis bruon.

It's nice, no?

PRISCILLA

It is.
But it hasn't worked, that idea. Common humanity. It's crap,
really.

KHWAJA

You are hard, niece.

PRISCILLA

I'm not, in fact. I wish I were.
What happened to your wife? Your little girl?

KHWAJA

My wife divorced me, in London, because she could. And my
sweet little girl is ashamed of me.
And I missed Kabul, where even the sale of a vacuum cleaner
part can lead to something interesting.
(Again holding out the poems)
17 Pindock Mews.

PRISCILLA

They told us in Islamabad not to accept letters, packages.

KHWAJA

They tell you all sorts of things. Official persons.

(Little pause. Priscilla takes the poems. Khwaja bows.)

KHWAJA

May the soul of your mother, awake or asleep, witness your generosity.

PRISCILLA

She would be surprised.
(She holds out her hand) I'm trembling.
I'm unused to exercise. I can't believe this day. It's as if there's more room suddenly, and air to breathe. Something snapped, or sprung loose. I can't tell you how uncharacteristic this is. Me, trudging about. She really would be surprised.
It's wicked to . . . enjoy this view, I should be back in the hotel room, grieving but . . . I've done that.
Years of that. Still, she's . . . dead. And considering what it's a view of. It's wicked.
If she was dead, there'd be her body. You can't lose a body.
(Little pause. She takes in the view)
Perhaps as they moved her body from one hospital to another, perhaps at every hospital they left some piece of her. So now . . . she's scattered all over Kabul. The whole city. It's her.

KHWAJA

Anything, everything can be lost.

ACT TWO

SCENE I

The hotel room. It's dark.
Milton is sprawled asleep atop his covers, fully dressed, the phone next to him.
A figure in a green burqa enters. She switches on the lights.
A muezzin's call for evening prayers, amplified through a loudspeaker, comes through from outside.
She goes to Milton, looks down at him. She sniffs.
She sees the empty bottle, picks it up, brings it close to her face-grille, reads the label, upends it: empty.

PRISCILLA

Where did you get this?

(Milton sits bolt upright, looks at the figure in the burqa and SCREAMS, leaps out of bed.)

MILTON

Get out! Get out! Wrong room! Wrong room! Please, please leave me alone!

(As he is screaming the figure is saying, "Dad, Dad!" as she removes her burqa. It's Priscilla, wearing the headphones, discman strapped around her waist.)

MILTON

You half startled me to . . . Skulking about like a panto ghost.
Are you *insane*?

PRISCILLA

Oh, watch that. Don't want to get into all that.

MILTON

Yes, well, insane, I might be speaking hyperbolically, loosely,
not precisely with regard to your particular . . . particulars,
but I have been alone, here, *worrying. For hours*. You're the
one ought to be watching herself, should you feel yourself
slipping. It's not a bit like home.

PRISCILLA

Yes, I know, unlike you I have actually bothered to go out
and have a look at it.

MILTON

No clean hospitals here. Mentally ill women get Toyota-
trucked to the old soccer stadium, I shouldn't wonder, and
(Makes a throat-slitting gesture) . . . pfffffffffffffft.

PRISCILLA

Enjoying yourself? Fantastic, two years have passed and
you've never mentioned it and you decide that *now*? *Here*?
Finally, you—
You're drunk.

MILTON

And you have a past record of mental affliction.

PRISCILLA

I attempted suicide.

MILTON

Which I believe is accounted a sign of—

PRISCILLA

Lots of people attempt—

MILTON

Lots of people are crazy, Priscilla, that proves—

PRISCILLA

I don't have to *prove* anything, Milton.
(Studying Milton for a moment, then:)
You're attacking me because you're horrified to think she might still be alive.

MILTON

She isn't.

PRISCILLA

Where's her body then? Her corpse? Why don't we have it?
(Beat)
I wasn't crazy, I'm not crazy. I was upset.

MILTON

Upset?! Upset causes people to overeat! Or to paint their hair and shove pins through their nipples! Upset people don't destroy themselves.

PRISCILLA

I was eighteen, I was stupid, so I, so I swallowed pills and—

MILTON

Many, many pills.

PRISCILLA

Yes, many many many pills. And—
Oh what a pity. And I was having such a lovely day.

MILTON

Upset! Stupid, yes, absolutely, I grant you stupid.

(Little pause.)

PRISCILLA

I needed time to, a place with close solid walls and an utter absence of the two of you. And *you* certainly stayed away. The electroshock was just dramatic effect, I agreed to it to punish you two.

MILTON

It was effective.

PRISCILLA

Was it? I was in there for months. You never visited once. The nurses remarked.

MILTON

Left hospital two years ago and has steadfastly refused to move out, yet in this ghastly place you stay out all day.

PRISCILLA

Not that you care but the hospital wasn't so very clean. Nicer of course than the places I saw today but then even the National Health looks good compared to—

MILTON

None of us ever recovered.
She went to see you in hospital that night and she never returned. Not really. I mean she returned, home, but . . . What should I have said. What was there to say?

(They look at each other. Priscilla shrugs. Little pause.)

PRISCILLA

I saw horrible things today. A hospital where—

MILTON

Please *don't*.

PRISCILLA

Horrible. But it was *me* there, seeing it, *me*. I thought, what kind of person watches herself seeing such things? Conceited, yeah? But I watched. I did, conceited, so what, doesn't matter. Them, these women, suffering. And me, there in the room with them, proximate. I . . . marveled at that. I marveled at myself. Ooh, Priscilla! Priscilla Ceiling in Kabul! Embarrassing. Never really done that before. Marveled. All day, I've felt like laughing. Inappropriate.

MILTON

When you were a girl you laughed all day.

PRISCILLA

No, inappropriate. I learnt it from her. How to be wrong on any occasion. Her weird forgotten words, yeah? *Murder* the conversation: "I'm suffering from psychopannychy." That'd stop a casual chat. If I asked what it meant—what's it mean Mummy, what's it mean—she'd shake her head.
Psychopannychy—it means: the all night sleep of the soul.
I looked it up. Daughter of a dictionary, me.
Who has a mother who says such things? She gave—nothing—and so she . . . demanded interpretation. She was so unyieldingly secretive, she felt if she shared anything, I'd become her. Maybe it wasn't ever rejection, just an invitation to understand?
She's finally . . . *acted*. She's made her move. D'you see?

MILTON

I'm afraid I don't know what you're talking about.

PRISCILLA

I know what they said, but . . .
The twilight outside, it's . . . powdery. Everything feels close here, the air, the mountains, not crowding in but there's . . .

well, proximity. Intimacy. Perfume. Like stepping into her clothes closet.

I have this feeling.

MILTON

You have entirely too many feelings.

PRISCILLA

Is she dead? She isn't dead.

SCENE 2

The next morning.
Priscilla in her burqa enters Khwaja's small room.
She removes the burqa, looks around.

KHWAJA

I am so pleased to have you visit my home.

PRISCILLA

It's small.
Shouldn't we be out looking?

KHWAJA

Perhaps you should sit.

PRISCILLA

No, I'm all jumpy, I dreamt all night. I want to go out.
(Opening and holding out the guidebook) Take me there.

(Khwaja looks at the page.)

KHWAJA

Cheshme Khedre. *(Shaking his head no)* It is a minefield.

PRISCILLA

We'll have to be careful, then.
You see, here in the book. She's marked it. "The Grave of Cain."
That would appeal to her.

(She starts to exit the room.)

KHWAJA

No such place exists.

PRISCILLA

It does.

(She thrusts the guidebook at Khwaja, who takes it and squints closely at the map.)

KHWAJA

There is here a, a smudge. *(He thrusts the guidebook map toward her)*
Do you not see what it is?

(She takes the book from him, looks closely.)

PRISCILLA

It's a question mark?

KHWAJA

Yes. This says, not "Grave of Cain," but rather, "Grave of Cain?" She was pursuing a rumor. On no official map is there ever a question mark. This would be an entirely novel approach to cartography. The implications are profound. To read on a map, instead of "Afghanistan," "Afghanistan?" It would be more accurate, but such an accuracy as might discombobulate more than mere geography and make the hierophants of all fixed order dash madly for cover.

PRISCILLA

It's difficult to believe that someone with, I dunno, your vocabulary? Would need to beg.

KHWAJA

I am not begging, I am providing a service to you.

PRISCILLA
Yes. Sorry. The minefield, please.
It's where they told us she was murdered.

KHWAJA
Might you consider? One more packet of poems for—

PRISCILLA
And then you'll take me to the . . . ?

(She takes the poems. Khwaja nods in thanks.)

KHWAJA
Last night several hours after I had left you at your hotel
I was approached by a gentleman who knowing that I have
been employed as your mahram asked me to convey to you a
message.

(Pause.)

PRISCILLA
What message? I don't know anyone in . . .
From . . . ?

KHWAJA
Let us go to this gentleman.

PRISCILLA
I'm going to black out.

(Priscilla sits suddenly. She stares at him.)

PRISCILLA
Where is she?

KHWAJA
She wishes you to know that she is not dead.

PRISCILLA

Give her back!
Fucking liar! She's . . . *Dead!*
What am I doing here? Who *are* you?

(Little pause. Khwaja starts to speak.)

PRISCILLA

I'll fucking murder you if you say another word, you cunt.

SCENE 3

Milton and Quango in the hotel room. The next morning.

MILTON

I didn't sleep. Or rather I did but I wish I hadn't. No more scotch?

QUANGO

Drank the lot yesterday. Sorry.
I've got opium.

MILTON

Opium?

QUANGO

Fancy sharing a bowl?

MILTON

You mean . . .
Opium?

QUANGO

Nangarhar Tarballs. Afghanistan's select, haut de grand cru etcetera premiere deluxe.

(Little pause.)

MILTON

Are you a dope fiend, Mr. Twistleton?

QUANGO

I'm not, no. Well all right I am a bit of an opium addict. But there's the tradition, you know, Coleridge, DeQuincy, Crabbe, Keats, Southey, Shelley, Byron.

(Little pause)

Oh all right then, heroin. I'm a junkie. Yes. Why else would I be here? Afghanistan supplies the world.

I came to do good, biscuits and bandages and woolly blankets. Heroin was a great surprise.

They must suspect, the Trust back in the U.K., I stay though they reduce my pitiful hire every year, what with donors drying up, Taliban fatigue, or disgust, rather. Ban-ban Taliban.

MILTON

So . . .

So the embassy in Islamabad, I am trying to comprehend this, has remitted my daughter and myself into the care of a heroin addict.

QUANGO

I hope this will not diminish in your eyes my prospects as a potential future son-in-law.

That was a—

MILTON

Have you . . . Please tell me the truth. Have you *looked* for my wife? Or don't you actually spend your time away from here . . . ?

QUANGO

Shooting up?

I've been to Avicenna Hospital, the Red Crescent HQ on the river, the Ladies Hospital at the College of Medicine or rather what used to be the College of Medicine, the U.N. offices or rather what used to be etcetera, the old Christian Cemetery

on Shahabuddin Wat, this morning in fact, to see if there was evidence of recent burial. There wasn't.
Your daughter was there.

MILTON

Priscilla.

QUANGO

With a Tajiki cicerone.

MILTON

Was she all right?

QUANGO

Under the burqa, hard to say.
Would you like me to leave?

MILTON

What is it like, opium?

QUANGO

Nausea at the get-go, then itching, usually, then . . . Peace. Immense dreams. Huxley, Freud, the Duchess of Windsor, it's got a pedigree.

(He hands a ball of opium and a pipe to Milton, who holds them, staring at them.)

MILTON

How much would it—

QUANGO

Oh no, no, no, I'm not . . . selling it, Milton. I . . . It's like a toddy. Truly. Helps sleep come.

MILTON

Might not be compatible with the nivaquine. Don't want to come home with malaria. I've had to stop taking my antidepressants because they interact poorly with the nivaquine, which is a pity because, well the circumstances recommend . . .
I mean she's out to drive me mad, Quango.

QUANGO

She seems, well, enduring, without illusion.

MILTON

(Shakes his head no) Wrong-o, laddie. Dustmotes and moonbeams from her head to her toes. And like most fairy princesses she is astonishingly cruel.
(Little pause. He rolls the ball of dope between his fingers as he talks)
That I should say such things about my daughter seems . . .
(He shakes his head) And to a stranger.

QUANGO

A stranger and a dope fiend.

MILTON

And a dope fiend, yes!
She attempted suicide.

QUANGO

Ah. Well, that is of course personal, um private—

MILTON

She shouldn't remain here is all. She's been in hospital. Some school chum she fell in love with, desperately in love, apparently, she's that kind of girl, he did a runner, and she . . .
She forced me to come. First the one throws away her life and then the other, competing with one another as always: "Me too, me too!" But why must they seek *my* blood?
She thinks her mum is still alive.

QUANGO

On the other hand, to most people, "your mum is dead"
more or less *defines* unacceptable, right?
She sounds um, a romantic heroine, rather. Or at least . . .
Well she seems vivid enough to me.

MILTON

(A smile, teasingly) So you keep saying.
Her name is Priscilla.
Opium is a vegetable derivative, is it not?

QUANGO

Bitter milk of the poppy plant.

MILTON

(Whispering conspiratorially) You won't share this? That I've
told you?

QUANGO

(Whispers back, playing along) I've got no friends.

MILTON

And yet you seem a bright, agreeable chap!
It relaxes you.
I could do with some relaxation.

QUANGO

As anyone can see.

SCENE 4

In Zai Garshi's hat shop. Priscilla, Khwaja and Zai Garshi.

ZAI GARSHI

Your mother, she wish you to know, she is not dead.
She wish you to know: she have not been killed by anyone,
all this is, ah, invented. She is happy, having met a gentleman. Some heavenly star-spangled night. She have spoken
the kaleema . . .
(To Khwaja, in Dari) Dar zabahnay Inglees-see cheest— *(What
is the English for—)*

KHWAJA

(To Priscilla) The kaleema. It's something equivalent to the
Nicene Creed, but shorter, for Muslims, to say it is to convert.

(Little pause.)

PRISCILLA

My mother is a Muslim?

ZAI GARSHI

Just so! And now she shall marry to a pious Muslim man of
means.
She wish to remain in Kabul, not to see you nor the father of
you, her husband of the past.

(A beat.)

PRISCILLA

This is . . . This is nonsense. I'm not fucking stupid you know, I'm SORRY we treated you so wickedly back in, when was it, 1879, but I'm not fucking AMERICAN, *we* didn't fire missiles at wherever it was, YOU NASTY FUCKING PIG, WHERE IS MY MOTHER WHERE IS SHE?

(She hits and slaps Zai Garshi, who shouts in Dari to Khwaja:)

ZAI GARSHI

Aya oh deewan'ast?! Khoh cherah chup nishastee? *(Is she crazy?! And why do you sit here saying nothing?)* OW! *(To Priscilla, in English)* It is truth it is truth I am telling you, stop!

(Khwaja pulls Priscilla from Zai Garshi and holds her till she stops struggling.)

PRISCILLA

Okay, stop, for a moment please.
My mother would never, never . . . do any of this, anything like this, this man is lying and you're lying and I'm being lied to.

ZAI GARSHI

I am unfinish.
In exchange that this man keep your mother as wife of his, he wish you to help remove now-wife of his who is crazy, first wife, she wish to go away, to London preferably. I arrange meeting of you with crazy first wife. You and this lady leave Afghanistan. Your mother, these have her wish.

(Little pause.)

KHWAJA

The man your mother marries already has a wife, who has gone mad, as many women have in Kabul. Your mother will live in place of this other woman, who will go to London.

ZAI GARSHI

Precisely.

KHWAJA

This man can no longer live with his wife. Her powerful family agree to emigration, because all want her gone.

ZAI GARSHI

This so-angry woman, as you will see.

KHWAJA

But divorce they oppose.

ZAI GARSHI

She have been a librarian, this lady, Mahala is her name, you will enjoy meeting her.

PRISCILLA

Oh do shut up, my God, shut up. Are you an idiot? Just . . . please.
Why won't my mother see me?

KHWAJA

I cannot answer that.

(Little pause.)

PRISCILLA

I am going to the police.

KHWAJA

That would lead to the arrest not only of this man, and of myself, but also several others who might be killed. The Taliban do not like being lied to, and this is an international embarrassment. If you will remain calm we—

PRISCILLA

CALM? What in God's name can you possibly mean by that? NO NO, I shall go to the police, I'll go to my dad in the—Oh God Oh Christ I don't know what the fuck to do, I don't know what the fuck to do, I'm getting out of here, I'm getting OUT of this *unbelievable place.*

(She tries to throw on her burqa, only getting entirely tangled in it.
She drops it to the floor, then stands, frozen.)

ZAI GARSHI

(Quietly) If I may speak. *(Pointing to Priscilla's discman, and speaking with reverence)* In the yellow Sony disc player is Frank Sinatra thirteenth album from contract of he with Capitol Records, fateful "Come Fly with Me," yes? Nelson Riddle-wallah, Axel Stordahl-wallah, Heinie-Bean-wallah?

(Priscilla is looking at the discman. She opens it, looks at the CD.)

ZAI GARSHI

You can take my word for it baby.
Some few of these LPs my parents may they have the perfect happiness of Paradise have leave to me when they are dead, some I have myself to buy at souks in Egypt, Ashkabad, Tashkent, Alma-Ata, airplane tickets to romantic places, yes? But those days and nights like painted kites they went flying by. And after Najibullah and Sibgatullah Mujadeddi and Dostum and Hekmetyar comes the Taliban, yes? They go to extremes with impossible dreams, yes? And so my record player is smashed and all each of the LPs of me, *Popular Frank Sinatra Sings for Moderns . . .* Slips through a door a door marked nevermore that was not there before. It is hard you will find to be narrow of mind.

KHWAJA

He was an actor. The Taliban have closed all theaters, all acting is forbidden, photographs are forbidden, all representation is sheerk; to make one thing that is like another might lead one to say that some things are like Allah, and nothing is like Allah. So the actor sells hats.

ZAI GARSHI

She also have love for Sinatra, your mother, she have with her pacooli hats and guidebook, marked "Grave of Cain," which she searched in Cheshme Khedre. It is all correct yes? Now she is appropriate Muslim lady in hejab, she will hear music never after, as the Taliban insist. She miss this musics already, your mother. She have great love for musics.

PRISCILLA

She did?
(Little pause)
Tell her . . . Tell her I want to see her.

(Little pause. Zai Garshi looks at Khwaja, who stares fixedly at Priscilla.)

ZAI GARSHI

I will convey.
I was promise that I shall have this LP, ah, *CD*. This is payment for message as I have convey.

PRISCILLA

She can tell me that herself.

ZAI GARSHI

Yes, please, but—

PRISCILLA

Until then, fuck off.

ZAI GARSHI

I would only want to hear. Please.

KHWAJA

It would be an act of kindness.

PRISCILLA

I'm not feeling . . . *Oh for God's sake.*

(She hands Zai Garshi the discman. He looks inside. He closes the lid.)

ZAI GARSHI

(Softly, deeply moved) Ah beautiful song that will not die, stardust of yesterday, music of years gone by. Who may solve its mystery? Why shall it make a fool of me? Beg God for strength they say, but something gotta give. 'Round and 'round I go, down and down I go, like leaf in the tide, to this earth of blood and *(In Dari)* tan haw yee. Loneliness. Guess who sighs these lullabies through nights that never end? Only the lonely know.
(He puts on the headphones)
'Scuse me while I disappear.
(He presses the play button. He listens, eyes closed, and starts to sing "Come Fly with Me":)

> Come fly with me, let's fly, let's fly away,
> If you can use some exotic booze
> There's a bar in far Bombay.
> Come fly with me, let's fly, let's fly away,

PRISCILLA

(Over this, after he's started to sing) And this woman, we're supposed to . . . I don't understand. My mother. Is this the shop in which she purchased the pacoolis? You have seen her. I mean . . . She's . . . well?

ZAI GARSHI

(Continues from above:)

Come fly with me, let's float down to Peru.
In llama-land . . .

(In Dari) Kabul, Kabul, aaah, kabulay maqbool oh dost dash-
taney yam, aaaaah, aaaah, bakoojaw burdandat, aw rayso-
wah showkaytay too mawraw may kushad . . . *(Aaaah, my
Kabul, my beautiful beautiful Kabul, where have they taken
you, aaaaah, aaaah, my longing for you is killing me . . .)*

*(Khwaja comforts Zai Garshi, then removes the headphones,
pushes the stop button, and hands the discman back to Priscilla.
The two Afghans hold each other.)*

PRISCILLA

What? What did he . . . ?

KHWAJA

(A finger to his lips) Ssshhhhh.

PRISCILLA

Take me to my mother.

SCENE 5

Mahala is in a rather elegant room, seated on a chintz-upholstered sofa. Priscilla, Khwaja and Zai Garshi stand. The men shouldn't be alone with these women; they're nervous, afraid.

MAHALA

Where are the women of Afghanistan? Can you tell me this? Ces gens parlent Pashto, ces etrangers, ces occupants, ces Talibani; Kabul speak Dari. Vous le saviez? Ce sont des nettoyeurs ethniques. *(These people speak Pashto, these strangers, these occupiers, these Taliban; Kabul speaks Dari. Did you know this? They are ethnic cleansers.)*

KHWAJA

(Translating haltingly, a few words behind Mahala, starting after "parlent Pashto") These people speak Pashto, these um . . . strangers, these occupiers, these Taliban. They are . . . ah . . . *(In French, to Mahala)* Nettoyeurs ethniques?

MAHALA

They seek to . . . destroy all who are not Pashtun.
(In Dari) Een haw khod raw Mullaw maygoyand, manzooram Ulamaw ast, een haw khod raw dar shawlay payombar paychawneeda, refugee camp gutter rats az Jalalabad wa Qandahar may auyand, walay een haw bah ferosh-ay taryok wa mawod-day mukhaderah, wa ba kushtar-ray atfal

maypardawzand, wa ba dushmanawnay-shawn reshwah may dehand taw bahonhaw zameenah-ay moowahfaqeeyat raw barroyay on haw muyahsar sozand. *(They call themselves mullahs, the ulema, they wrap themselves in the Prophet's mantle, these refugee-camp gutter rats from Jalalabad, from Khandahar, but they sell drugs and murder children and bribe their enemies to give them their victories.)*

KHWAJA

(Translating, overlapping) They call themselves mullahs, the ulema, they wrap themselves in the Prophet's mantle, they are from the camps, and from Jalalabad, from Khandahar, they sell drugs and murder children and bribe their enemies to give them their victories.

MAHALA

Atrocities they commit. People are flayed alive. The skin remove, yes? Yes! Bake to death lock in metal trucks in the desert. Thrown down . . . Des sources. Wells. And where is America?

PRISCILLA

I . . . I'm from the—

MAHALA

(Continuous from above) The CIA posylaiet denezhnyie sredstva etim ubliudkam cherez Pakistan, gdie vooruzhionnyie vlasti, c'est tout les Pashtuni-wallah, sumasshedshikh i terroristov, auf die eine odere andere Art werden sie an den Tueren alle ihrer Herren erscheinen, but still Se She Ah platit im den'gi, posylaiet im oruzhiie. *(The CIA sends these bastards funding through Pakistan, where the military high command, it's all Pashtuni-wallahs, these madmen and terrorists, they'll turn on their masters sooner or later, and still the U.S. pays them money and sends them guns.)*

ZAI GARSHI

This lady says CIA pay the Taliban through Pakistan. I personally do not—

MAHALA

America buys this, bombs, from Communist Chinese to sell in secret to Taliban through Pakistan. Afghanistan kill the Soviet Union for you, we win the "Cold War" for you, for us is not so cold, huh?

PRISCILLA

I'm not—

MAHALA

(Almost continuous from above) The gas pipe of Unocal! For U.S., yes? Il faut subir le Taliban so all must be calm here so gas . . . *flows* to ships, for American profit, to . . . to . . . Afin de vaincre L'Iran! Pour que les États-Unis puissent régler un compte de vingt ans avec L'Iran! *(So that Iran can be bested! We must suffer under the Taliban so that the U.S. can settle a twenty-year-old score with Iran!)*

KHWAJA

(Translating, starting after "Afin de vaincre") We must suffer under the Taliban so that the U.S. might settle a twenty-year-old score with Iran.

MAHALA

(Not waiting for Khwaja to finish) You love the Taliban so much, bring them to New York! Well, don't worry, they're coming to New York! Americans!

PRISCILLA

I'm English.

MAHALA

English, America, no difference, one big and one small, same
country, America say, Britain do, women die, dark-skin
babies die, land mine, Stinger *projectile*; British, American so
what? So what you say?!
Trente mille veuves habitent la ville, trois cent milles enfants
à nourrir, et le travail leur est défendu! À la bibliothèque on
donnait aux mendiantes du pain et du thé, qui-est-ce-qui
leurs en donne maintenant? *(Thirty thousand widows live in
the city with three hundred thousand children to feed, and
they're not allowed jobs! At the library we would hand beggar
women bread and tea, who gives them bread and tea now?)*

KHWAJA

(Translating, after "à nourrir") There are three hundred thousand widows and children who may not work. *(After "on donnait")* At the library they gave away tea and bread. She wor-
ries now that . . .

MAHALA

(Not waiting for Khwaja) They have close library! Library!
This is Islam? Muslims are les gens du Livre. Scholars! Poets!
Les peintres, les compositeurs, les philosophes, les mathé-
maticiens, nous savions comment marchait l'univers des
siècles avant vous, nous avons inventé l'énumeration et le
zéro et la médecine! Et ils ont fermé la bibliothèque! *(The
people of the Book. Painters, composers, philosophers, mathe-
maticians, we knew how the universe worked centuries before
you did, we invented counting and the zero and medicine. And
they've closed down the library!)*

KHWAJA

(Translating, after "avant vous") And Muslims have been
through history educated people. We were once in advance
of the West in knowledge. *(After "bibliothèque")* So the
Taliban have closed down the—

MAHALA

Le Quran ne suffit pas! *(The Quran is not enough!)*

(Khwaja indicates to Mahala that he won't translate that.)

MAHALA

The Quran these cannot read! Illiterates and child murder-
ers. Nettoyeurs ethniques. Suray char, seporahyay noh
(Arabic: surah four, chapter nine): "Let people fear the day
when they leave small children behind them unprovided."
(In Dari, to Khwaja and Zai Garshi) Wah too khodraw mard
may donee? Shomaw ranj may barayd? Maw ham bayshtar
ranj may baraym? Shomaw een hawlat raw bar-r-r mardom
nayah'wardayd? Shomay jon yon wa washeeyon wa shomaw
atfal-ay ton raw az gurusnaygee nah maykushayd? Shomaw
een raw eejawzah nah maydehayd? Kee eenraw eejawzah
maydayhad? Ayah shomaw fekehr maykonayd een Islamast?
*(And you call yourselves men? You suffer? We suffer more. You
permit this? These criminals and savages to enslave and
oppress your women? To make your children starve? You
allow this? Who would allow this? You think this is Islam?)*

PRISCILLA

(To Khwaja) You stopped translating.

KHWAJA

She is railing at us. She calls us effeminate men.

MAHALA

Not "effeminate," this I do not say. I say women are braver
than you men of Kabul. Queen Gawharshad rule half the
world from Herat. Malalai insist to you: kill the British
invaders, she insist and so then you do, because she, *she* have
the courage. Young girls have march and die to fight communist and the Russian soldiers, but you, you do not die, you do
not march, nothing from you while we starve in rooms,

because these "heroes," they make you feel like not pious Muslim, because you want a coward order, *le fascisme.* I go mad, British, I cannot cease shouting all day, a bird, a bird taps the window, I shout at these bird, *"Die, break your neck at the glass!"* I am so bitter of . . . of . . . De L'Âme? L'esprit?

PRISCILLA

Spirit? Soul?

MAHALA

I pray to God let all birds of the air be curses to fall on Kabul with dead eyes and broken necks. Je suis bibliothècaire! Je veux me promener encore une fois. Je veux aller en soirée encore une fois. Je n'ai rien à lire! *(I am a librarian! I want to walk down the streets again. I want to go to parties again. I have nothing to read!)*
Des femmes, elles se meurent tout autour de moi, je les entends mourir dans leurs maisons quand je regarde furtive-ment par la fenêtre, quand je me promène dans ma burqa. Ma cousine, sa fille, elle s'est pendue. Ma vieille amie Ziala Daizangi, Hazarra de Bamiyan, s'est jetée du toit de—*(Women are dying all around me, I can hear the sounds from the houses when I peek out the window, when I walk in the burqa. My cousin, her daughter, she has hanged herself. My old friend Ziala Daizangi, Hazarra from Bamiyan, threw herself from the roof of—)*

KHWAJA

(Translating, after "soirée encore une fois") She wants to . . . *(After "je n'ai rien à lire")* She is a librarian. She wants to go out and to parties. She has no books to read. *(After "fenêtre")* She hears women die, sounds of this come to her from, from . . . *(After "Bamiyan")* Her cousin hanged herself and—

MAHALA

Ziala Daizangi, she I have known thirty forty years? Hazarra family from Bamiyan, the family of she now in Qetta, refugee camps. This one dies, that one starve, that one exploded, shot, rape, rape, die, die, die, die, die, whole family, whole family of she, all Daizangis of she, husband of she, children—*she throw herself off roof*! Taliban not to permit burial and I cannot go to see the body of my friend, my family afraid, no mahram will come and her body, what did he do? Her uncle? There are dogs in the street? Ziala body have been left in the street for dogs? In my dreams, always, she does not come to me, her body is in the street, as it fell. I miss . . . I miss . . . *(She weeps)*

(Pause.)

ZAI GARSHI

Usually she is cheerier.

PRISCILLA

(Lost, not knowing what to say or do) Do you want to go to London?

KHWAJA

Her passage papers through the tribal areas, her exit visa across the Khyber Pass to Pakistan, these have been pre-pared. A sponsorship letter would bring her into the British embassy in Islamabad. English chap . . .

PRISCILLA

Mr., um Twistleton?

KHWAJA

He has such a letter.
You must decide.

PRISCILLA

Your husband . . . has married my mother. Is this true?

(Mahala weeps, hides her face, and rocks.)

PRISCILLA

You've actually . . . seen my mother? Alive? Today?

(Mahala crawls on all fours to Priscilla, grabs her hand, kisses it. Priscilla, horrified, tries to pull her hand away. Mahala will not let go, holding onto Priscilla's fingers.)

PRISCILLA

Please, please don't.

MAHALA

To leave is a terrible thing. But I must be saved. Yesterday I could not remember the alphabet. I must be saved by you.

(Priscilla pulls her fingers from Mahala's grasp.)

SCENE 6

Evening. Priscilla and Milton in the hotel room. Priscilla, deeply shaken, leans against a wall of the room for support.

PRISCILLA

All day in the street, I've heard her, running. Well in my head I did. Just ahead of us, always just around the corner. You know your mother running, you know that sound. Nearer I came, the more rapidly she'd run, out of sight, my proximity . . . repelled her, drove her on, on, away . . . I wasn't looking for her I was *hunting* her I felt. It was so much like home. She simply couldn't bear to be near. So it's not inconceivable, is it? Alas alas alas alas alas. She is . . . alive.
(She looks at her hand)
She really bruised my hand. So that I wouldn't forget her. She's stronger than she looks.
It's hard though, to imagine it, isn't it? The clothes she'd be wearing now, the strange food she'd be eating—Mum, I mean. All Afghan dusty, getting darker. The bed she'd be lying in at night. Her, not knowing the language, that's hardest of all. Maybe it's the not speaking that appealed to her, or.
Or getting on without us.
Don't know about you but *I* feel a proper ruddy fool.
Milton?
Hello?
Please, say something.

MILTON

I've been smoking opium with Quango and it doesn't agree with me.

(A beat.)

PRISCILLA

Oh you have not.

MILTON

She is dead.

PRISCILLA

She needs us.

(Little pause.)

MILTON

I've smoked opium. It was pleasant at the time, though it's disagreeable, after. I dreamt of an iron-banded oaken chest full of gold and I fucked it, in my dream. I shan't try opium again, I feel a bit wonky now, I had what felt like a, like a . . . an orgasm deep inside my head, and now I want to go home. Your poor mum. We were incompatible but I did grow to love her. And she's dead, well, it cannot be comprehended. I want to do as she would have me do, Priss, I want to watch over you, to . . . help. I want you to stay, here, with me, in this room, quiet and calm, and tomorrow, you and I will *leave*.

PRISCILLA

Be a *little* brave, Dad.

MILTON

No, but I'm not brave and I've never been and know what? I've no wish to be! You see? None! Never have! LET! GO! Do you think she—what? In secret collusion with these men, that mullah, that doctor, with Reuters for Christsake, she invented that horrible death so that . . . simply so that she could vanish? It's mad! And, and, she . . . *married* a Muslim? Which, allow me to point out, she might just as easily have done in London, and a nice Western sort of Muslim too, not one of these . . . barbarians. So that she can spend the rest of her life in what must never have been more than a Himalayan bywater at the best of times, draped in parachute sheeting stirring cracked wheat and cardamom over a propane fire? I mean no doubt she was *tired of me* but . . . And why concoct this hoodoo of disassemblage? They might simply have said she was shot, or stepped where she oughtn't to have stepped, or for that matter she could have called and said, "Hullo, I have met a desperately gorgeous Afghan chappie and I have become his umpteenth wife and sod you lot, you will see me no more a-punting down the Thames." These people who are the ruthless creatures of a culture, if I may call it that, a culture of betrayal and brutality and dissembling, are practising on you, they see you as . . . vulnerable. If I weren't here with you I've no doubt you'd fall for the whole jabberwocky and would be arriving at our flat tomorrow with some Afghan lady whose name is composed entirely of gutturals and sounds like a toilet backing up, "Here's Mrs. Wargarwazbaz Bizooli Waza, Dad," then you'd help her unpack her—what is it? *Burqa?*

PRISCILLA

Go fuck an oak chest, Milton.

MILTON

Let her rest, for pity's sake! The poor woman! Not enough you . . . Yes! You drove her here, wasn't me, you tormented us both, and and drove her to, to *madness* and now you pursue her dead through the streets of this hellish city demanding . . . *WHAT, PRISCILLA?* What do you want from us? To rescue you? Rescue yourself, for God's sake! Or you'll be mis-

erable and lonely the rest of your life! Look at yourself! What
man conceivable would want to marry you?

I'm sorry.

I'm still . . . drunk. Or—

PRISCILLA

When I took those sleeping pills I was pregnant.

(Little pause.)

MILTON

I didn't know that.

PRISCILLA

Not a lot you did know, eh Milton?

MILTON

I didn't know.

PRISCILLA

Killed the, the fetus.

Good we're not Catholic. Is it a sin, if the killing's oops unin-
tentional? Oops. Dead. Oops. She could have been Catholic.
Calvary was always before her, suffering for those she saw
suffer. Useless.

She moved all this, didn't she, out of the house, out from
under all that crying in the kitchen nights when nobody
could hear and into the great world beyond where people
who hate one another . . . *murder.* We're far beyond fathers
and daughters and all that. *You* look, look what she's done,
where she's brought us. We're at the stage of blood sacrifices,
right? And and sorry about the progeny, Dad. But why should
there be more like us?

MILTON

I didn't know you were going to have a baby.

Oh Priss. I'm, I'm. Oh Priscilla, I'm . . .

PRISCILLA

She knew. I told her and told her. She just . . . couldn't talk about it. All those words, but not a one for me.

(She goes to him. She hugs him. Milton gently pushes Priscilla away.)

MILTON

When we return, your mother's life insurance, and her bank account, it's a goodly sum, you may have it all, I'm sure she'd wish it. And I would like you to take it, and move elsewhere.

PRISCILLA

You're throwing me out.

MILTON

I'm asking you to leave. Yes. I think it's for the—

PRISCILLA

But *why*? You can't. She's died, and—

MILTON

Ah yes but she's not dead, you see. Stay here. Seek her out. Tomorrow morning Ariana will fly me out or I will take a taxi to the Khyber Pass if they aren't flying. And I think you must go, don't you? Don't you think so? What's left now? You hate me.

PRISCILLA

I don't.

MILTON

You have made it clear. Or perhaps you don't, I . . .
She was gentle, you are ungentle. Perhaps you can find a husband here, you as well.

(Priscilla picks up the burqa, puts it on.)

MILTON

Oh for fucksake, don't.

PRISCILLA

It's what you want.

MILTON

It isn't.

PRISCILLA

Well *I* want it. Whatever else is out there, I don't care anymore, *I* want it.

(Priscilla exits, slamming the door.)

SCENE 7

Later. Milton and Quango in the hotel room. Quango holds a square of tinfoil, which contains a small lump of white powder—heroin—over a cigarette lighter. Milton, guided by Quango, sucks the smoke rising from the heated powder through a straw. When Milton inhales, Quango indicates that he should draw the smoke deep into his lungs and not exhale. Milton does, and is flying immediately.

QUANGO

Off you go, Milton. Star of your own movie, you are, flying carpet over minarets in the moonlight.

(As Milton is enjoying his rush, Quango turns to the junkie's apparatus he's laid out for himself. As he speaks he lights a candle in a holder, then shakes powder from a packet into a spoon, carefully.)

QUANGO

They say the Taliban all have purloined videocassette players. The buggers are particularly fond of *Titanic*, you know, "Leo, Leo . . ."
Theirs is a landlocked country, but if anyone should be able to understand the metaphor of a ship foundering, it's the Afghans.

(Holding the spoon over the candle)
Heroin stanches sentiment. I thought it so simple when I first arrived, Man A wants X, and why Man B denies him, and I shall help them both. 'Tisn't . . . simple, you'd have to be God, look down on Afghanistan, high up hallucinatory cinematoscope: "Turn it turn it, night and day I do that—I am God but . . . No way out for the Afghans." Pakistan over there, supporting the Taliban, give them Afghanistan as a distraction from their *real* dreams—

MILTON

What are *real* dreams?

QUANGO

What? Oh, the *Big* Dream: Pashtunistan. The Pashtuns of Afghanistan and their near-relatives, the Pathans of Pakistan, dream of creating it by joining Afghanistan with Pakistan's North-West Frontier territory. Major worry for Pakistan, that.

(Quango ties a cord around his upper arm, palpates the vein, shoots up.)

MILTON

Ouch.

QUANGO

No, it's . . . Yin and yang. After the yin pinch, puncture, there's . . . mmmm . . . Lovely.

MILTON

It is lovely. Heroin is far superior to opium.

QUANGO

Not as lovely now as it was in the beginning.

MILTON

Like marriage.

QUANGO

I'm a bachelor. And fantastically lonely.

MILTON

No lovely or at least cooperative girls about?

QUANGO

None. Well, whores, but sad, shabby whores, the real girls, all locked away, shrouded like . . . like . . .

MILTON

Like shrubbery against the frost!
Do you realize . . . I actually said the word "fuck," meaning copulation, right in front of my own daughter. Is it the drugs, or do you think I might still be in shock?

QUANGO

Or maybe you're just a rubbishy old git.

(They laugh. Milton is growing giddy.)

MILTON

If I am it is you who have made me, Traitor-Angel! Spirited Sly Snake! So get thee gone!

QUANGO

Where shall I go?

MILTON

Pashtunistan!

QUANGO

Can't do, it doesn't exist.

MILTON

Let us establish it!

QUANGO

Pakistan would not approve.

MILTON

Well *fuck Pakistan*, then!
Been wanting to say that for *years*!
Nice juicy bite out of Pakistan, would it be? Pashtunistan?
And Pakistan is not large.

QUANGO

No.

MILTON

(Doing Nöel Coward) India is large.

QUANGO

Yes.

MILTON

India is . . . *enormous.*

QUANGO

Yes it is. So the Pakistanis keep the Taliban with Afghanistan
and plans for Pashtunistan lay by. But the longing for it poi-
sons the region: the Taliban export their desperation. Turn it
turn it. This way it's Pakistan, that way Shi'ite Iran, and the
Sunni Taliban slaughtering the Shi'ite Hazarras, pleasing
Sunni Pakistan and Sunni Saudi Arabia and their overlord
the sunny United States which has smiled down on the
Taliban until—

MILTON

(Giggling) Until last week when America bombed them! *(Laughing)* It's down the rabbit hole!

QUANGO

Killed quite a number of people actually. Ten, twenty-eight, forty-eight, a hundred and eight, depending on the source.

MILTON

(Laughing!) Osama bin Laden!

QUANGO

No, they missed him.

MILTON

(Laughing!) Opium farmers, then!

QUANGO

Not in the desert, Milton. You're, uh, spoiling my high. Have you noticed, nearly every other man you meet here is missing pieces?

MILTON

(Proud of this) I've not left this room since we arrived!

QUANGO

Reagan was right about them, they are . . . the bravest people on earth. Have you noticed their remarkable jade-colored eyes?

MILTON

I thought you said heroin stanched sentiment.

QUANGO

I'm in love with your daughter.
I am.

MILTON

You only saw her once!

QUANGO

And yet.

MILTON

Naaaaaaah you're not, you want to roger her, but be warned: she is fertile and then she bombs the innocent inhabitants of her womb with sleeping pills, because, as I said, she is not at all *lovely*. Leave the dead in their graves! But she will disinter. She's a born digger, she was born with a spade in her hands. The little ghoul. *(He starts to cry)* My wife has died, horribly died, and she chooses NOW! NOW! Can you *imagine*?! To tell me this! Her own father! That she aborted! And I don't know why I am so full of, of RAGE, I could, I could give a fuck, babies, you know, I could give a fuck about babies! But . . . She . . . it's the abandonment or betrayal or . . . Ah Christ. I am unmarried! I'm . . . alone! What'll I do? What'll I do now when I'm home?
(He shudders)
I must lie down. Queasy all of a sudden.
(He does)
Don't think I'll discuss family matters no more, me, I'm . . . *Really* dizzy.
(He begins to drift off)
Sing me a song of Pashtunistan, far, far away . . .

QUANGO

There is no song to sing.

MILTON

(Nodding out) Have they coffee crops in Pashtunistan? Anything to export, labor for . . . pentium processor chip assemblage, or . . . ?

QUANGO

Poppies. An oil pipeline . . .

MILTON

Something like that, golden, golden . . .

QUANGO

(Soft, singsong) From Kazakhstan and Uzbekistan, from Turkmenistan through Afghanistan, oil flowing to Pakistan, and never through Iran, nor Moscow nor New Delhi, golden energy from the Caucasus to the sea, to Western free democracy, past ghostly Pashtunistan alive only in the heart's plans of every Taliban man and each Pathan . . .
(He sees Milton has gone to sleep)
Ah, Milton? You do not care for the geopolitical?
Lord Emsworth was looking through the wrong end of a telescope at a cow. "It was a fine cow, but like most cows it lacked sustained dramatic interest."
Wodehouse. Apex of Western Civilization.
(He looks around the room. He goes to Priscilla's suitcase. He opens it)
I suppose I could sniff her knickers, or put on her bra or something.
Have a wank.
(He roots around in the suitcase. He finds a bottle of pills. He holds them up and gives them a shake)
Antimalarial? Antidepressant? Abortifacient?

(He pockets the pills. He removes a pair of Priscilla's panties. He sniffs them, then puts them on his head. He puts his head in the suitcase, then slips a hand in his pants and tries to get hard, have a wank. The door opens and Priscilla enters in her burqa, quietly. She takes in the scene: Milton unconscious on his bed, Quango with his head in her suitcase, doing something nasty.)

PRISCILLA
(To Quango) What the fuck are you doing?

(Quango sits bolt upright, panties still on his head. He freezes, she freezes, staring at one another. Then she pulls off her burqa, as he yanks the panties off his head. He stumbles over

to gather up his shooting works. She shoves her clothes back in her suitcase. As this is going on:)

PRISCILLA

(Shoving clothes in the suitcase) Oh God, you . . . You were in my . . . You . . . Jesus. What the fuck were you two . . . Jesus.

QUANGO

(Scrambling to pick up his works) I'm . . . *(He giggles, mortified)* Blame it on the drugs, please, I do such stupid things when I'm stupid and—

PRISCILLA

GET OUT!

(Quango turns to leave.)

PRISCILLA

You have a, a . . .

(Quango stops.)

PRISCILLA

I've been told you have some official letter? If I wanted to get someone from here to London, you have a—

QUANGO

You're not serious. For, for the, the Afghan lady who . . . ? Your dad says he won't agree to—

PRISCILLA

Oh, so he told you. About . . .

QUANGO

Yeah.

PRISCILLA

Chatterbox, him.

QUANGO

He is that, yeah.

PRISCILLA

(Overlapping) They said she knows people in London.

QUANGO

They always say that.
In Islamabad they'll run checks and, you know, to certify she's not a terrorist. And you're, ah, unemployed, that'll make it harder to—

PRISCILLA

How do you know that? That I'm unemployed?
What else did he tell you?

QUANGO

Um, only that your mum is . . . that you *think* she's . . .

(Milton, still asleep, sings: "You meet a girl and find out later/ She smells like a percolator . . ." from "The Coffee Song.")

QUANGO

I was helping him relax.

PRISCILLA

You succeeded.
(Gesturing toward her suitcase) You relaxing too?
He's shattered, you shit. His wife is . . . He's destroyed.
You'd *no* right to give him . . .
You do not inspire confidence, "Quango."

QUANGO

Dave.

PRISCILLA

"Quango."

QUANGO

Yeah.
It's a formal intro letter, we keep them in a locked file at the
Finnish Compound. They're valuable. Political Refugee Status.
Gets you through Peshawar to the embassy at Islamabad.
The first step of a steep staircase at the top of which is London.
And who would not want to ascend?
I'll trade it you.

PRISCILLA

Trade it.

QUANGO

You might not give a fuck but should she turn out to *be* a terrorist, it'd be *my* name on her permissory letter, do considerable damage to the trajectory of my, ah, career, that would.
But for a toss? A tumble? For the—

PRISCILLA

You're joking.
Are you out of your—

QUANGO

Yes. Yes. Definitely yes. Bit too long in the sun. Desperate? In
love? Desperate in love? Yep. It's me. You seem like the best
shot in forever, not a, a lady journalist or a, you're, well I figure it's unlikely but fire away, that's the motto of the Twistle-
tons, that is, just—

PRISCILLA

Just give me the fucking letter, Dave.

QUANGO

Fuck you I shan't. Sorry. I mean, sorry about it all, your . . .
horrible da and, your mum, who by the way is *dead*, I mean,
I don't mean to be vicious but everyone dies here, fatal place
really, sort of house special, death is. Here have a drink of
water: typhus, dysentery, malaria, diarrhea, ready-for-it
rimshot: Death! Another bone-load for the Christian cemetery. She must've intended it, a woman? Flying to Kabul
alone, for a lark? Face it for fucksake, she *topped herself. I'm
sorry but she bleeding did.* Suicide. This, ah, proclivity for
oblivion, it runs in your family, eh?

PRISCILLA

He told you?

QUANGO

Or, or rather—

PRISCILLA

He told you.

QUANGO

she got some poor Afghan street sods to do her topping for
her—

PRISCILLA

About my . . .

QUANGO

and—

PRISCILLA

And what else?

QUANGO

But if, but if you've no more love of yourself and your bloody
easy life than that, if you don't care to be alive at all, why

scruple at anything? If you're just throwing yourself away, couldn't you have sex with me first? Am I worse than dying?

PRISCILLA

And what else? What else did he—

QUANGO

The abortion. That.

(Pause.
She stares at him. He looks everywhere else.)

PRISCILLA

(Quiet, confused, sad) But he . . . All that?
But I'm his daughter. And he doesn't even *know* you.

(Another pause. Then she goes up to him and kisses him, a deep long kiss. He stands frozen still while she does it.)

QUANGO

Please. Stop. I'm . . . sorry.

PRISCILLA

You're a junkie, right? Needles? Are you clean? Well never mind, I wouldn't believe you, have you got condoms?

QUANGO

I . . . Yes.

PRISCILLA

One condom.

QUANGO

Yes.

PRISCILLA

God you're really desperate. I'm . . . worse.

(She puts the burqa back on and heads for the door. She stops and turns back to him.)

.

PRISCILLA

Well?

QUANGO

Nights like this I know I'll never get clean. More than likely die in Kabul.

You've made me so lonely, Priscilla.

PRISCILLA

No doubt.

Pretty fucking lonely myself, Dave. Orphan now.

I guess you lead the way.

(He goes out, she follows.)

ACT THREE

SCENE 1

So late at night it's nearly dawn, but the sky is still black and wild with fierce stars.

An open place, mountains of rubble. Terrible fighting took place here.

There are signs posted warning of the danger of undetonated mines.

There's a depression in the ground, a rectangle of cleared earth outlined in small white stones, about five feet long and a foot and a half wide. A flame in a pot burns at one end. Near the flame pot, a basin with water and a towel.

Khwaja enters leading Priscilla, who is in the burqa, by the hand. They are silent and move with great caution, stepping very deliberately: land mines.

KHWAJA

We're here.

(Priscilla takes off the burqa. Khwaja examines the plot of earth outlined with stones. It is terribly cold. When they speak they are quiet, glancing around, aware of the danger.)

PRISCILLA

(Looking up, softly) Oh my God.

KHWAJA

What is it, did you—

PRISCILLA

Look up there! Look at that sky! Black! Black! Those stars!
Crikey. We could be on the moon! Oh sweet Christ it's . . .
Unearthly!
(She turns to Khwaja, sings to him) "Around the world/
I searched for you/I traveled on when hope was gone/To keep
a rendezvous."

KHWAJA

(Over the above, on "hope") Sssshhhhhhhhhhhh . . .

PRISCILLA

(Continuing over his "sshhh," but softer) "I knew some way,
somewhere, somehow/dadeedah dum, dadeedah dum . . ."
There. See? Poetry. Kabul has changed me. I've listened.
(Looking at the sky again) It almost hurts to look at them,
they're so bright, it's like . . . holes in your brain. That's the
Milky Way, isn't it? The heavens!

KHWAJA

This is a minefield. The Taliban patrol the area. There is a
curfew.

PRISCILLA

Sorry.
This is Cheshme Khedre?

(He nods.)

PRISCILLA

It's where she was killed.

KHWAJA

Or not.

(Indicating the rectangle of stones, the depression in the earth)
It seems we have found what you sought. This is a grave.

(Khwaja kneels by the grave.)

PRISCILLA

Whose?

KHWAJA

(Shrugs) I do not know. Adam's first son?

(Priscilla doesn't know what he means at first; a beat, then:)

PRISCILLA

Oh.
He'll insist on leaving in the morning, my father. If he's
conscious. I'm sorry, I had to come here. I can't go home
empty-handed. Maybe there'd be some sign here for me, that
she'd marked the map for me. Maybe if I came, she'd . . . be
nearby and meet me. Stupid, I know, but . . . I suddenly want
her, more than I can ever remember. Is she . . . ? Do you
know where she . . . I leave tomorrow. I'll leave her here. Can
you . . . ?

KHWAJA

(Indicating the flame) Someone has been praying at the grave.

PRISCILLA

Who?

KHWAJA

I do not know.

(She goes to the grave, kneels, looks at it, then:)

PRISCILLA

(Disappointed) Who'd pray to Cain?

KHWAJA

Perhaps they pray *for* him?
A legend holds that he founded the city.

PRISCILLA

Cain? Well that makes a certain sense.

KHWAJA

Yes. He was many years older than a thousand years old when he arrived. His heart was worn out with regretting, after so many centuries of remorse, it must have been. And Kabul has always been welcoming of strangers, weary travelers. Even so, it was a great mistake, burying him here. Unlucky man. Unlucky city.

PRISCILLA

Yes.

KHWAJA

Lucky to leave an unlucky city.

PRISCILLA

Yes.

KHWAJA

And Mahala?
When you appeared on my doorstep at such an uncivilized hour in the company of Mr. Twistleton, I hoped you had obtained the permissory—

PRISCILLA

No. I asked him to bring me to your . . . He would've given it, but . . . I didn't ask for the letter.
I'm only here by accident, it's my mum's fault I am, I shouldn't be.

KHWAJA

And yet here you are.

PRISCILLA

Oh, Jesus, would you *stop*?! You, watching me, I've seen you, you ask me to take this stranger to London and . . .

KHWAJA

(Softly, under her) It is not I who have asked you to . . .

PRISCILLA

(Continuous from above, right over Khwaja) . . . and then, and then, oh here, these *poems*, and what next, packets of white powder?

KHWAJA

Ssshhhh . . .

PRISCILLA

I can't help you, her—*look at me!* Half the days I can't manage *myself*, I can't just . . . *take* her. Think what you're asking. *(Hard)* No one will save her. She'll just . . . die. She's just one of the people who dies, and no one minds.
(Little pause)
We've brought our misery to your city, my family. I'm sorry.

KHWAJA

(Angry) What have you ever brought us besides misery? Gharbi? Ferengi? The West? And many among us would like to give your misery back to you.
(He stands to leave)
You have to take home with you nothing but the spectacle of our suffering. Make of it what you will.

(Khwaja starts to walk away. Priscilla remains by the grave, on her knees. Khwaja stops. They don't look at one another.)

PRISCILLA

(Pleading) I don't know if she's alive or dead. People go missing, everywhere on earth but that's no help to me. I don't
know . . . what we meant to one another, and she's gone now,
and that's true too, everywhere on earth but . . . again, no
help to me. Will I see her again?
She could write something, then. Or, or she could see me.
(She's crying) This is cruel.

(A beat. Khwaja turns to her. She turns away.)

KHWAJA

She will not write. She says she is an Afghan now and shall
not write or speak until her hands become hands that write
Dari and Holy Arabic, until she can recite the Suras by heart
and his kisses have changed her mouth she will neither write
nor speak. Not to you, especially not you. You are a danger.
She loves you too much. Don't hold her back from traveling.

PRISCILLA

You mustn't embroider. Or I'll think you a liar.

KHWAJA

I am a poet, it is not possible that I lie.
She has told him to tell you this: you have suffered and will
suffer more yet, she fears, because your heart which is a loving
heart is also pierced through. She prays now to Allah who for-
gives all who sincerely repent, to forgive her and through her
penitential loneliness, to forgive her daughter as well.

PRISCILLA

She . . . To forgive me. For . . . ?
Oh I don't understand. That she came here . . . For me? Is
that what . . . ?
Well perhaps. Perhaps that's so.
If she is alive, or, or if she is dead.
Tell her I said she shouldn't have gone, but. Tell her I said
good-bye.

(The light is changing, night giving way to dawn. A muezzin's call for prayers.
Khwaja and Priscilla finally look at each other; he breaks the look first, apparently slightly disoriented.)

KHWAJA

I should go. To the mosque for dawn praying.

PRISCILLA

Yes.
Pray for me.

(Khwaja bows. Priscilla kisses the earth of the grave.
She stands.
She hands Khwaja the discman.)

PRISCILLA

Please give this to Mr. Garshi. His recompense.
(She takes a twenty pound note from her pocket)
And for you.

(Khwaja receives it, bows. He produces another sheaf of papers.)

KHWAJA

One last packet of poems for Mr. Sahar.

(Priscilla takes the poems.)

PRISCILLA

17 Pindock Mews.
Your poem, the one you recited?

KHWAJA

Yes.

PRISCILLA

I didn't ask. What did it mean?

KHWAJA

It is very simple. It is about someone waiting in a garden, in the snow.
Deep within, someone waits for us in the garden. She is an angel, perhaps she is Allah. She is our soul. Or she is our death. Her voice is ravishing; and it is fatal to us. We may seek her, or spend our lives in flight from her. But always she is waiting in the garden, speaking in a tongue which we were born speaking. And then forget.

PRISCILLA

A tongue.

KHWAJA

A mother tongue. A language we must strive to learn again.

PRISCILLA

How? Learn it how?

KHWAJA

We spend of what we love. Through *zakat*. We give to one who has not.
(In Arabic) Hafazakee Allahu ala al-dawaam.
May God keep you in His embrace forever.

PRISCILLA

I don't understand.
Oh God.
Oh fuck I can't believe I'm . . . Oh all right. I have the letter. I have the permissory letter. You *people*, it's . . . Tell Mahala. Tell her we leave half eight, a taxi to the Khyber Pass. I can't be blamed when it all goes wrong.

KHWAJA

Go home with care.

SCENE 2

Milton and Mahala are sitting in a desolate concrete room. There is perhaps a barred window with mountain peaks visible outside, or perhaps they are visible outside the door. A Taliban Border Guard is also present, also sitting. He has a Kalashnikov and ammo belts. There are a few boxes of papers, and on the walls, lists of government edicts and quotations from the Quran in Arabic.

Milton is frostily polite to her but terrified. Mahala is working hard to attract his attention.

MAHALA

But please. To explain to me. Computer . . . ah—

MILTON

Network engineering. Well, all right then, imagine a number of people in a darkened room—this is a metaphor, it's hard, very hard to find the right metaphor and I don't—at any rate, people in a darkened room, each has a torch, or, or a lantern, many different lanterns, each with a different colored flame. The electromagnetic spectrum—including the visible rainbow as well: color is a perceived property of frequency, thus-and-so-many pedahertz . . . Or is it terahertz? Well, ten to the fifteenth or ten to the eighteenth, it's . . . Let's see. It's hard to explain.

MAHALA

We say: "We have taken the coloring of God, for what better hue is there?"

MILTON

Do you, now?

And let us say that it is my task to sort them all, these people and their lanterns, who aren't people but—well, in order to, to *banish confusion*, to send him here, send her there, through this or that door, well, that is what I do. Now how do I do this?

In my work, we have things which we call "duals."

MAHALA

Duals?

MILTON

Pairs of two things which are alike but also opposite. Frequency is one thing, it occupies the dimension of space. And time is another, the opposite of space—and yet in computer network engineering, these two opposites may be looked at as a dual, a, a single thing, in that information, language, may be sent along either the long axis of time, one thing following another, or along the short axes of frequency and amplitude, height and width. I . . . very seriously doubt that I am making myself understood.

MAHALA

I do not understand.

MILTON

No I'd think you wouldn't. It's an unforgiving place, science. If you don't speak its language it spits you out peremptorily.

MAHALA

It is I who have failed. My English. Years of not speaking . . .

BORDER GUARD

(In Pashtun) T'bayaday ekhpul chahdaree pah sar klay. *(You should put on your burqa.)*

TONY KUSHNER

MAHALA

(In Pashtun, fierce hiss) Moolsah! T'dah chardare pah sar kah! Kalakhar! *(Drop dead! Put on your own burqa, you shit head!)*

(Little pause.)

MILTON

What did he say?

MAHALA

He ask if I shall like a glass of water. I tell him I did not. He is so polite boy.

BORDER GUARD

(In Pashtun) Tamawmay mardhawyay Inglees kooneeastand. Ekhpul mah shookatah dah woowayah. *(All British men are homosexuals. Tell your boyfriend that.)*

MAHALA

(Overlapping, in Dari) Birow-woo dohborah saray kish'zorat day konay Pakistanee. *(Go back to the farm, Pakistani peasant.)*

(Little pause.)

MILTON

I'm sorry you know, it's not that I don't want you to come to London. My daughter isn't well and she'd no business offering. *(Little pause)* She believes my wife has married your husband.

MAHALA

I am told this, yes.

MILTON

My wife is dead. She was killed.

121

MAHALA

I am not told this. I am told she, my husband, marry. I am told.
I . . . am needing to come to London.

MILTON

Pakistan might have to do. You have papers to get through
the border, but. London.

MAHALA

Refugee camps in Peshawar. No one, no one care to see that
this one, that one has dead. *(Wrong word)* Death. *(Wrong
word. She's frustrated)* Parlez vous français? Deutsch?

MILTON

English is my only language, alas.

MAHALA

English, and, ah, *science*.

MILTON

Pardon?

MAHALA

You speak *science*.

MILTON

(Surprised!) Oh! Yes.

MAHALA

"Duals."

MILTON

(Surprised! Seeing her!) Duals! Indeed. I'd no idea you were—

*(The voice of Mullah Durranni is heard, and then he enters. He
is now wearing military clothing. Milton and the Border Guard
stand.)*

MULLAH AFTAR ALI DURRANNI
(To Mahala, in Pashtun) Munzh-tah parwah neshtah cheh chertazeh. Angleezee injalai seh asnod cheh deh Afghanistan day Islami Imawrat marboo tadah warsara dah. Ow haghah dah waw kawee cheh asnodo deh haghah la boxna relah shawneedah cheh woorsarah oos neshtah. *(It doesn't matter to us if you leave or where you go. The English girl has papers belonging to the Islamic Republic of Afghanistan. She claims they were stolen from her luggage. They are not with her.)*

(Pause.)

MULLAH AFTAR ALI DURRANNI
(In Pashtun, with menace) T'khawmakhaw bayad mawtah za wab raw klay! *(You must answer me!)*

MAHALA
(In Dari) Agar man bakhshawyesh az shomaw jenawbay Mullah saheb. May khaw ham shomaw bawyad khaw he sheh maw raw qabool conayd. *(If I ask for mercy, Minister Mullah Sahib, you must grant it to me.)*

BORDER GUARD
(In Pashtun) Mullah saheb, haghah khazah droghjana-dah. *(Mullah Sahib, she is a liar.)*

MILTON
Might someone tell me what's going on?

MULLAH AFTAR ALI DURRANNI
Have you remove or witness to be remove from chest . . . *suitcase* of your daughter a, a paper? Many paper?

MILTON
Visas? We gave them to Mr. Twistleton in Kabul, on behalf of the British government, he authorized the—

(Mullah Durranni holds up his hand for silence, and Milton stops talking.)

MULLAH AFTAR ALI DURRANNI
Other paper.

MILTON
For . . . You mean for her? But you see, we aren't responsible for—

MULLAH AFTAR ALI DURRANNI
(Again the hand) Other paper. Not visa. Strange language paper.

MILTON
I don't know what you're talking about. May I see my daughter, please? I would like to see her now.

MULLAH AFTAR ALI DURRANNI
Soon, please, sit.

MILTON
No, not soon, this has gone on long enough, for two hours we've been sitting here, now please bring her here to me or bring me to her or—

(Mullah Durranni sweeps out of the room, and as he leaves he nods to the Border Guard who ratchets some ratchet on his Kalashnikov. Milton sits.
The Border Guard sits.
Pause.)

MILTON
(To Mahala) Do you think she's all right?

MAHALA
I think we shall be very quiet.

MILTON

Do you know what papers he's talking about? What are "strange language papers"?

(Little pause. Then talking again, very scared)

In a sense, strange languages is what networking is about. Languages expressed as binary code, numerical sequences, ones and zeroes, digitally reducing the unmediated slovenly complexities which exist, let us say, analogically in space, by making of complicated nuanced things their simple non-nuanced identicals, which exist not in space but in space-frozen-and-rendered-sequential, in time, one nothing one nothing nothing one, you see. I'm afraid I rattle on when I'm, well, afraid.

MAHALA

(Hearing something familiar) One nothing one nothing nothing one? Sequences of codes of numbers, as with for example the Dewey Decimal System?

(He looks at her with considerable surprise.)

MILTON

In a sense, yes.

MAHALA

(Making the connection) By which knowledge is to change to les fiches de reference, to numerals, which . . . metaphor, represent?

MILTON

Yes, yes, just so! But how improbable! How do you come to know of the Dewey Decimal System?

MAHALA

International for libraries.

MILTON

You're a librarian?

MAHALA

I have been being for vingt, ah twenty year, librarian.

MILTON

Ah, yes? "Où est la bibliothèque?"

MAHALA

Ah bon, très bon, mais j'avais l'impression que vous ne parliez pas français? *(Oh good, very good, but I thought you didn't speak French?)*

MILTON

No, no, it's the sum total of my first form French, "Où est la bibliothèque," I've no idea why I said it, um—*urge* to communicate, I suppose. In our dire straits. I'm . . . Hah! Quite a good deal less frightened than I'd have thought I'd be. Kabul has emboldened me.

MAHALA

Bold, yes. Kabul. Lion.

MILTON

Mr. Dewey, he was . . . some sort of philosopher, was he not, American?

MAHALA

Ah, no, the Dewey Decimal System, *Melville* Dewey. You think, ah, *John*, John Dewey, great . . . prophet, philosophe, America progress? Utilitarienne! Religion and, um . . . *reason*, the mind—the soul and the *mind* he says are not in . . . *opposition* with one another but ah . . . *C'est a dire* . . . *(She searches for the word, gestures two things merging)*

MILTON

Conjoined.

MAHALA

Oui! Yes! Alike, opposite! A *dual*!

MILTON

A dual! Yes! Very very good!

MAHALA

(Getting it!) Ohh enfin: these which is seem not alike, *you* shall make a single thing! To, to *communicate*!

MILTON

Well, that is in fact what networking is, that's what I do! Energies, languages traverse a passing-through place, a, an . . . intersection.

MAHALA

Intersection. Like Afghanistan.

MILTON

I don't . . .
Oh. Yes. *Precisely! Precisely!* Afghanistan! *That's* the metaphor! Armies, and, and gas pipelines and even Islam, communism, tribes, East and West, heroin, refugees, moving chaotically, and each is a language.

MAHALA

And you shall . . . make machine making to banish confusion?

MILTON

Well, for starters, this will interest you, my company voluntarily participates in a libraries computerization scheme, you know, anyone who has a computer, can, with the touch of a button, peruse, well, *millions* of books I should think.

MAHALA

Millions of books? Not possible.

MILTON

Day or night, everything ever written, there at your dining table with the flick of a—

(Milton sees that Mahala is crying.)

MILTON

Oh, I'm sorry. Why are you . . . ?

MAHALA

Poor Afghanistan.

(Priscilla enters, wearing a headscarf, carrying the burqa, looking haggard.)

MILTON

Are you all right?

MAHALA

(To Milton) Please take me to London.

MILTON

Priscilla?

(Priscilla shakes her head and shrugs, indicating: "I don't know.")

MILTON

You haven't been harmed?

PRISCILLA

(Indicating Mahala) This isn't about her Milton. They don't care about—

MILTON

Are we going to be released? Can we call ahead to—

PRISCILLA

(To Mahala) It's about the fucking poems.
Did you—

*(Mullah Durranni comes back in. The Border Guard stands
again. A second armed Border Guard appears.)*

MULLAH AFTAR ALI DURRANNI

(To Priscilla) We shall want again to search the suitcases.

PRISCILLA

(Moving away from Mullah Durranni, afraid) I would give
you the bloody things if I knew where they were. Why do you
want them?

MILTON

(Overlapping with Priscilla) What poems?

PRISCILLA

They're in *Esperanto*, for fucksake, they're of no use to
anyone!

MILTON

(Overlapping) What are you talking about? Esperanto poetry?
Why do you have Esp—

PRISCILLA

They were given me.

MULLAH AFTAR ALI DURRANNI

Gift?

PRISCILLA

Is there an export tax on . . . Yes. Gifts.

MULLAH AFTAR ALI DURRANNI

To . . . to read?

PRISCILLA

I guess so.

MULLAH AFTAR ALI DURRANNI

Do you know this . . . Espre . . . What shall you call it?

PRISCILLA

It's . . . What difference does it—

(Mullah Durranni raises his hand.)

PRISCILLA

Put your hand down. I'm not afraid of your fucking hand.

MILTON

Priscilla, unnecessary antagonism is—

PRISCILLA

Esperanto. Oh God this is so stupid.

MULLAH AFTAR ALI DURRANNI

You speak this . . . Esperanto?

PRISCILLA

(Simultaneously with Milton) I do, yeah.

MILTON

(Simultaneously with Priscilla) Of course not. No one does.

MULLAH AFTAR ALI DURRANNI

(To Priscilla) Speak it please.

(Priscilla is silent.)

MILTON

No one speaks Esperanto, not anymore. I would really like to know what this is about.

MULLAH AFTAR ALI DURRANNI

(Sternly, to Priscilla) You have hire this Tajik mahram. He is said to have give you papers. Written in language so no person can read, these papers you are to give to person in London. These papers are not of poems but Tajik informations for Rabbani and Massoud. Placements of weapons and this. Written in . . . *(To Mahala, in Pashtun)* Shefer? *(Code?)* Code? How it's said?

(Mahala doesn't look at him.)

MULLAH AFTAR ALI DURRANNI

They have tell you this woman is wife of Muslim man, Kabuli man who have marry dead British woman, she have not die. *(To Milton)* Yes?

MILTON

It's . . . Do you know where my wife's body is? Why has it not been found?

MULLAH AFTAR ALI DURRANNI

This woman is Pashtun woman, crazy woman, who she is? She is doctor wife, Doctor Qari Shah. *(To Mahala)* This is not so?

(Mahala looks at Priscilla, then looks down.)

MULLAH AFTAR ALI DURRANNI

You think Doctor Qari Shah marry your wife? You think he make story, whole story? Just for you? *(Indicating Mahala)* She have flee him, he may demand with witness she shall be killed. Useless woman. USELESS WOMAN!

(He nods to the Border Guard. He ratchets the Kalashnikov again. Mahala screams.)

MULLAH AFTAR ALI DURRANNI

(To Mahala, in Pashtun) Senadoona roklah. Zeh pohayzhoom cheh tah saradah. Kah raw naklay, woo bad day wazhnoom. *(Give me the papers. I know you have them. Give them to me or I will have you killed.)*

(He advances on her, screaming at her; she slouches out of the chair onto the floor, covering herself with her burqa, sobbing.)

MULLAH AFTAR ALI DURRANNI

(In Pashtun) Maw tah raw klah os! Maw tah raw klah os! OS! OS! OS! *(NOW! NOW! NOW!)*

PRISCILLA

(Overlapping) Oh my fucking God, he's—

(She runs at Mullah Durranni. The second Border Guard shoves her to the ground.)

PRISCILLA

He's going to kill her, MILTON, STOP HIM!

MILTON

(Loud, terrified) I have over two thousand pounds. Please do not kill her. I will give you all the money I have. Let us go. We don't have your papers. My daughter knows nothing of any of this, this is your problem entirely, not ours. Here. *(He takes out his wallet and proffers it)* Here. Take. Please do not shoot this woman.

(Mullah Durranni stares at the wallet, then at Milton, for a rather long time. No one moves.)

MILTON
I . . . I am asking you, sir, to please allow us to take her with us, and to leave. We really don't know where . . . Please.

MULLAH AFTAR ALI DURRANNI
You ask me to take baksheesh. Wog take baksheesh, yes? This is crime in Afghanistan. You shall put this away.

MILTON
You, you take bribes. I've been told, you people take bribes. This is a bribe. I've been told you're not so pure. This is a bribe. Take it, please. I don't mean to insult you, sir, but you can't shoot her.

MULLAH AFTAR ALI DURRANNI
You want her?

MILTON
I don't want to watch her die.

MULLAH AFTAR ALI DURRANNI
We shall shoot her in other room.

MILTON
Please. Take.

(Little pause. Mullah Durranni takes the wallet, throws it on the floor at Milton's feet.)

MULLAH AFTAR ALI DURRANNI
(Calm, quiet) Afghanistan is Taliban and we shall save it. No one else shall, no one else care. England betray us. United States betray us, bomb us, starve us to . . . *distract* on adulterous debauch Clinton and his young whore. *This* is good for woman? Islam knows what dignity a woman shall have. U.S. and Russia destroy us as destroy Vietnam, Falestine,

Chechnya, Bosnia. As India destroy Kashmir. As Tajikistan and Uzbekistan and Kazakhstan keep Islam from its people. As U.N. deny Taliban to be recognize. All plot against Islam. Iran plot against Islam. For five thousand years, no one shall save Afghan people. No one else but Allah may save it. We are servants of Allah.

(He goes to Mahala, crouches; almost whispering, in Pashtun:)

MULLAH AFTAR ALI DURRANNI
T'dah shayroonah lahray. Zeh baday loos kloom, ow b'ya baday pah goolay woo wah hoom. *(You have these poems. I will have you stripped and then shot.)*

(Mahala shakes her head no. She holds up her empty hands. Pause. Mullah Durranni looks at her.)

MULLAH AFTAR ALI DURRANNI
(Tired, giving up; to the Border Guard, in Pashtun) Zah lar-lashah ow deh haghah boxoona pah motor-keh watchawah. *(Go put their suitcases on the truck.)*

BORDER GUARD
(In Pashtun, pointing to Mahala) Dah bayad talashee shee? Munzh b'ya dah khazah deh dah talashee deh parah woogooroo, loy Mullah saheb. *(Shouldn't she be searched? We can get a woman to search her, Minister Mullah Sahib.)*

MULLAH AFTAR ALI DURRANNI
(In Pashtun) Zah bastanayoh pah lahree-kee watchawah. Haghah sarah asnoh doh nishtah. *(Put the suitcases on the truck. She doesn't have the papers.)*

BORDER GUARD
(In Pashtun) Khadah, magar-r-r— *(Yes, but—)*

MULLAH AFTAR ALI DURRANNI

(In Pashtun) Zeh cheh seh wayoom, haghah watchayah! *(Do as I tell you to do!)*

(The Border Guard exits.)

MULLAH AFTAR ALI DURRANNI

Doctor Qari Shah does not demand death of her, she is of nothing to any Afghan man. She shall die in sewer of Qetta or Peshawar, she shall not be for London. British embassy shall certainly refuse entry. *(To Priscilla)* You have lie to her.

(Mullah Durranni begins to leave.)

PRISCILLA

What . . . Please, what has happened to Khwaja Aziz Mondanabosh?

MULLAH AFTAR ALI DURRANNI

I know no such man.

PRISCILLA

To my mahram? To the Tajik mahram who wrote the . . .

MULLAH AFTAR ALI DURRANNI

(Harsh!) Tajik mahram have been arrested and executed. For treason against the Islamic Emirate of Afghanistan.
Truth is truth. We seek what has been revealed to the Umma, what is higher and more complete. May Allah forgive you and may you find your way to submit to Allah.
(Smiling but serious) If not, go to hell.

PERIPLUM

The room in the Khyber Pass dissolves. The sound of rain.
Stephane Grappelli's version of "A Nightingale Sang in Berkeley
Square" is heard through the rain. Milton helps Mahala stand,
remove her coat; he watches her as she adjusts her hair and
clothes, becoming a modern English woman. She looks very
different.
It's London. 1999.
In the Homebody's kitchen again, as in Act One, Scene 1,
Mahala is seated in the Homebody's chair, reading.
Priscilla enters in an overcoat.

MAHALA

Hello.

PRISCILLA

I let myself in.
I still have a key.

MAHALA

It has been a long while.
My English has meantime improved.

PRISCILLA

Are you sleeping with him now?

MAHALA

Your manner meantime has not improved.

It has been difficult for me. But it is lovely here.
(The book in her hands) I am reading the Quran again. For
all those terrible years, I was too angry. I am myself becom-
ing Muslim again. The Book is so beautiful, even in English.
In Arabic its beauty is inexpressible.
Please sit.

PRISCILLA

He wanted to shoot you. The mullah.

MAHALA

No. He did not. He is not so bloody as that. We, our families,
Durranni Pashtun, and he and my husband had been
comrades-in-arms. Mujahideen group Taraki-I-Talibani. I am
no farmer's wife, little Bibi Nobody. Since I was a girl, I . . .
intimidate everyone, and this perhaps has saved my life.

PRISCILLA

(Angry) I saved your . . .
Forget it.

MAHALA

Your newfound reticence becomes you.

PRISCILLA

Did he shoot Mr. Mondanabosh?

MAHALA

This I can't know, but it is likely, I fear.

(Pause. Priscilla starts to cry, then stops herself.)

PRISCILLA

I'm not going to ask you about my mother.

(Silence.)

MAHALA

I am lying, you think. I loathe the Taliban, they are my own people but I loathe them. You think I have lied to help bring from Afghanistan the poetry of Mr. Mondanabosh, which are not hymns of peace in dream language of universal brotherhood but military information for the Northern Alliance.

PRISCILLA

Who sound as dreadful, really, as the Taliban.

MAHALA

We hope not so. Better for women, not as God-crazy. Not agents of Pakistan. On the other hand, Massoud, Rabbani are Tajiks, not Pashtun, so will the Afghans follow them? *(She shrugs: Who knows? Then sadly)* Or will Afghanistan without the Taliban sink again into unending civil war, with missiles supplied by the West?
In Afghanistan, Priscilla, the choices are frequently narrow.

(Little pause.)

PRISCILLA

I know.
Sometimes I think they're what Afghanistan needs, the Taliban. Anything anything for certainty. I get the appeal of fascism now. Uncertainty kills.

MAHALA

As does certainty.
They're like the communists, the Taliban. One idea for the whole world. The Dewey Decimal System is the only such system.

PRISCILLA

It provides no remedy.

MAHALA

Only it provides knowing, and nothing more.
Vous m'avez sauvée, Priscilla. You have saved me.

(Little pause.)

PRISCILLA

As I have been saved.
I . . . tried to kill myself. Here. In this house. *(She gestures upstairs)*
I'm ashamed of that. After all I have seen. I'm so ashamed of that now.
I *need* to be forgiven.
I tried to leave. I was pregnant. I didn't want to be. I didn't want to be a mother. And one of us had to leave. Or both might have died. We . . . got lost in one another, somehow, frightening, to be so lost, so . . .
So she left.
I miss her. I love her. She was my mother. But . . . Can I say this?
In the space she's left . . . Some . . . joy? or something has been rising. Something unpronounceable inside is waking up. I . . . I've no words for this.
Psychopannychy. *(She laughs)*
In this house, I knew . . . I could hear her still.
Y'see Mum? One sharp goad from a terrible grief and . . . the soul is waking up.
(Little pause)
I should go.

MAHALA

I hope you will return.
It is lovely here.
I am gardening now! To a Kabuli woman, how shall I express what these English gardens mean?

Your mother is a strange lady; to neglect a garden. A garden
shows us what may await us in Paradise.

PRISCILLA

She read instead.

MAHALA

I have examined her library. Such strange books.
I spend many hours. The rains are so abundant.
In the garden outside, I have planted all my dead.

(As the lights fade, in the garden outside, a nightingale.)

END OF PLAY

AN AFTERWORD

When the Twin Towers collapsed I was standing on a rainy beach on the Dingle Peninsula in Ireland, watching my four-year-old niece and her newfound playmate, a little British girl, splashing about in a tidal pool. I noticed a crowd gathering around a nearby car radio; I joined it just as, in New York, the second tower was coming down. Minutes later, the beach was abandoned. Everyone went home to wait for what seemed like the end of the world.

The next day, as my sister and I tried to get back to New York (it took five days), I received emails from a few newspapers asking for an article about the attack. I imagine everyone who'd ever written anything was asked to write about the attack. I refused. I've never been shy about offering opinions, but opining felt hasty, unseemly and unwise. One of the papers was gathering short essay responses to the question: "What is the meaning of 9/11?" This on 9/12. I thought about the wisdom of Jewish laws of *shiva*, the weeklong period of silence, retirement, prayer mandated as one begins mourning. I didn't write.

A month later, as the cast of *Homebody/Kabul* was beginning rehearsals at New York Theatre Workshop and letters containing anthrax spores were arriving in newsrooms all over the city, I was asked to prepare a statement for the press, since it was assumed that, given the subject of the play, there might be controversy. This is what I wrote:

Homebody/Kabul is a play about Afghanistan and the West's historic and contemporary relationship to that country. It is also a play about travel, about knowledge and learning through seeking out strangeness, about trying to escape the unhappiness of one's life through an encounter with Otherness, about narcissism and self-referentiality as inescapable booby traps in any such encounter; and it's about a human catastrophe, a political problem of global dimensions. It's also about grief. I hate having to write what a play is *about*, but I suppose these are some of the themes of this play.

I didn't imagine, when I was working on the play, that by the time we produced it the United States would be at war with Afghanistan. My play is not a polemic; it was written before September 11, before we began bombing, and I haven't changed anything in the play to make it more or less relevant to current events. It was my feeling when writing the play that more arrogance, more aggression, more chaos and more bloodshed were the last things needed in addressing the desperate situation in which the Afghan people find themselves. I would hope my feeling is expressed in the play. It seems to me that Americans have shown, in recent weeks, a desire to know much more about Afghanistan. My greatest hope for a play is always that it might prove generative of thought, contemplation, discussion—important components of what I think we want from our entertainments.

We have been abruptly plunged into horror: by 9/11 first and foremost, by the incomprehensible yet inescapable fact that we are under attack by an unknown enemy using biochemical weapons, and by the actions, both here and abroad, of our own government. More horror is to come. We have been profoundly alienated from our "dailyness," from a certain familiarity and safety without which life becomes very difficult. It seems to me that one of the hardest challenges we face is to keep thinking critically, analytically, compassionately, deeply, even while angry, mourning, terrified. We need to think about ourselves, our society—even about our enemies. I have always believed theater can be a useful part of our collective and individual examining.

Eight months have passed. When we started rehearsing, the Taliban were still in control of most of Afghanistan; before the first preview, the Taliban had disappeared. The American bombing campaign in Afghanistan seems to have ended the Taliban theocracy, at least for the time being. And while the Air Force for the most part avoided striking Afghan cities, there are still no reliable figures for the number of casualties and fatalities in the current war in Afghanistan. If the first Iraqi war is any indication, reliable figures will never appear. Attempts on the part of the Bush administration to curtail constitutionally protected freedoms for U.S. citizens, disinformation campaigns and the like, have met with real resistance, suggesting a resiliency and enduring vitality among the watchdogs of our democracy, even in the face of widespread alarm. The public debate about the legitimacy of torturing prisoners has gone underground,[1] as has the anthrax scare and its subsequent investigation. Ground Zero is now as level as a parking lot.[2] What the U.S. intends for Afghanistan is anybody's guess. The fate of the people of Afghanistan is, again, in the hands of the U.S., and there are ominous signs that we are beginning to lose interest. The

1. This was written long before the second Iraq war began and before the news arrived from Abu Ghraib prison—though since then, the torture debate has again evaporated.
2. Now a gaping hole, which is probably how it ought to remain, since it is, after all, a grave that can never be closed.

countries responsible for the international force needed to keep order in the newly destabilized and still heavily armed country are already showing signs of wanting to withdraw. And a continued American presence in the region is unlikely to prove an unmixed blessing. Bush ran for president against the Clinton administration's record of "nation building." Hard to know what to make of his present posturing as the Simón Bolívar of Central Asia; one suspects an oil pipeline runs through it. His Pontius Pilatism in the occupied territories and his attempt, catastrophically late, to become a peace broker, are rather easier to judge.[3]

The play was written before 9/11. I'm not psychic. If you choose to write about current events there's a good chance you will find the events you've written about to be . . . well, current. If lines in *Homebody/Kabul* seem "eerily prescient" (a phrase repeated so often that my boyfriend Mark suggested I adopt it as a drag name: Eara Lee Prescient) we ought to consider that the information required to foresee, long before 9/11, at least the broad outline of serious trouble ahead was so abundant and easy of access that even a playwright could avail himself of it; and we ought to wonder about the policy, so recently popular with the American right, that whole countries or regions can be cordoned off and summarily tossed out of the international community's considerations, subjected to sanction, and refused assistance by the world's powers, a policy that helped blind our govern-

3. Again, all written before America's unilateral and criminal invasion of Iraq in 2003. In 2002, the Bush administration forgot to include a line item in its budget for securing and rebuilding Afghanistan; Congress had to scramble to add some money. The U.S. armed forces are still in Afghanistan, searching Ambushistan for bin Laden. The world's pledge of many billions to rebuild remains unfulfilled—and what was originally promised wasn't remotely enough. Today Afghanistan seems mostly to be back in the hands of the warlords who finished off what was left of Afghanistan in the post-Soviet civil war, several of whom are named in the play. Taliban-like Pashtun fundamentalism has assumed control of the government in Pakistan's Northwest Frontier Territory. Opium production is back, bigger than ever.

ment to geopolitical reality, to say nothing of ethical accounta-
bility and moral responsibility.

In addition to the requests to write something after 9/11,
I was asked to unwrite something. An editor of a magazine
to which I'd contributed a short piece, written before 9/11,
emailed to inquire as to whether I would like to remove a
sentence in the piece in which I called George W. Bush a
"feckless blood-spattered plutocrat" (more executions under
his belt than any other governor—any other elected official?
—in American history) and Ariel Sharon an "unindicted war
criminal" (the Sabra and Shatila massacres in Lebanon).
I saw no good reason to make the change. 9/11 may have
altered the world forever, and in the process it may have res-
cued the quasi-legitimate and already-teetering Bush administration, just as it gave new life to the deservedly dashed
career of Rudy Giuliani—some of the world's worst people
benefited from 9/11—but transformative as the event has
proven and will prove to be, nothing changes what has been.
The past can't be erased and can only be effaced if we agree
to forget, and what has been shouldn't be forgotten. People
change, I believe deeply in the possibility of people changing,
but *Bush*? *Sharon*? Eight months have passed and look at the
godforsaken mess the feckless blood-spattered plutocrat and
the unindicted war criminal have wrought in the Mideast.
Change requires as its catalysts and fuel both good faith and
decent intention, as well as deep need. Need, not greed;
decent intention, not oil profiteering; good faith, not ethnic
cleansing and military occupation cloaked in fundamentalist
misreading of Scripture. As Margo Channing reminds us,
"Everybody has a heart. Except some people."

If I may be permitted an aside: I know the preceding
statement will upset people who believe that the Palestinian
Authority, if not the Palestinian people, share equally in the
blame for the current nightmare in the Mideast, which
threatens the entire planet. I won't concern myself with the
fanatics and crazies who believe the Palestinians to be solely

responsible. But to the genuinely perplexed, among whose number I count many friends: I am an American and a Jew, and as such I believe I have a direct responsibility for the behavior of Americans and Jews. I deplore suicide bombings and the enemies of the peace process in the Palestinian territories and in the Arab and Muslim world. I deplore equally the brutal and illegal tactics of the IDF in the occupied territories, I deplore the occupation, the forced evacuations, the settlements, the refugee camps, the whole shameful history of the dreadful suffering of the Palestinian people; Jews, of all people, with our history of suffering, should refuse to treat our fellow human beings like that. I deplore the enemies of peace in Israel and in America as well, and to them, inasmuch as they are far more mighty, and already have what the Palestinians seek, statehood, I apportion a greater share of the responsibility for making peace. Israel must not be destroyed. The Palestinian State must be established. Peace talks must resume. Sharon must go. Perhaps Arafat should go too, if for no other reason than for the oppressive tactics he employed against his own people before the second intifada—but like Sharon he should be removed by the sovereign will of his own people. An international peace-keeping force should take hold of the situation, a condition Israel must accept.

What time in human history is comparable to this? It's nearly impossible to locate plausible occasions for hope. Foulness, corruption, meanness of spirit carry the day. I think a lot about 1939, of the time the Russian writer Victor Serge called "the midnight of the century," when women and men of good conscience, having witnessed the horrors of World War I, watched helplessly, overwhelmed by despair, as fascism and war made their inexorable approaches; as Leninism transformed into Stalinism; a time, when, in Brecht's immortal phrase "there is injustice everywhere/and no rebellion."

Great historical crimes reproduce themselves. One injustice breeds new generations of injustice. Suffering rolls on down through the years, becomes a bleak patrimony, the only inheritance for the disinherited, the key to history, the only certain meaning of life. Sorrow proliferates, evil endures, the only God is the God of Vengeance. Hope dies, the imagination withers and with it the human heart. We no longer dream, not as a people; we are instead demonically possessed. Confronted with the massacre of innocent people, we quibble rather than act; the death of children becomes a regular feature of our daily entertainment. Technology offers oppressor and oppressed alike efficient and cost-effective means of mass murder, and even acts expressive of dissent, defiance and liberation are changed by desperation, madness, the appalling progress of weapons development and the global arms market into suicide bombings, into brutal expressions of indiscriminate nihilistic mayhem.

The following speech used to be in the third act of *Homebody/Kabul*, which was, in its first draft, a very long play. It's still a long play but it used to be longer. This speech, about Cain, Adam's first son who is according to legend buried in Kabul, was whittled down to help bring the play into tighter shape.

Cain was marked, and so they drove him out, everywhere he tried to rest, they drove him away. Only Kabul did not. He was an extremely old man when he arrived, many years older than a thousand years old. Anyone could see that it was past time, that he was done for, that he could no longer hurt anyone. His heart was worn out with regretting, after so many centuries of remorse, it must have been. He most likely felt nothing at all by the time he arrived here, an animal looking for a soft bed of leaves, some place out of the night wind. And this has always been a hospitable city, welcoming of strangers, a good host to the weary traveler.

But still it was a great mistake. Letting him stop
here, burying him here. A great mistake.

They should have driven him away.

I was moved by the fact that the city of Kabul was Cain's
resting place. In the play I suggest that he was, perhaps,
murdered there. Over the centuries, so many people have
died in Kabul, in Afghanistan, the number of the slain in the
last four decades perhaps exceeding all those who had fallen
in all the centuries before. Cain was marked not as a sign of
the evil he had committed when he murdered his brother,
but as a protection: God warned the human race to leave the
murderer unharmed. He who killed Cain would be punished
sevenfold. Did Cain die violently in Kabul? Is the city in
some sense cursed? What is the genesis of evil, how far back
does one have to go to find it? Isn't the abandonment of
the futile and fatal search for lost originative causes one
place at which a distinction can begin to be made between
justice and revenge?

It is in fact only part of the legend that Cain died and
was buried in Kabul. The Homebody points out, citing
Nancy Hatch Dupree's guidebook, that Cain may have founded the city. This legend has a resonance with the passage in
the Holy Scriptures in which we are told that Cain's sons,
Jabal, Jubal and Tubalcain, were the human race's first musi-
cians and metalsmiths. There is attached to this destroyer,
this hunter, this solitary, desperate, cursed figure of ultimate
barrenness, some potential for that renewal of life which is
human creativity. Cain is the founder of a city as well as a
fratricide, the father of the arts as well as the first person to
usurp God's power of determining mortality, the first person
to usurp the role of the angel of death.

Tragedy is the annihilation from whence new life springs,
the Nothing out of which Something is born. Devastation
can be a necessary prelude to a new kind of beauty—necessary, perhaps, but always bloody. In the preface to his verse

drama, *Cain*, Byron tells us: "The world was destroyed several times before the creation of man." That makes a certain sort of sense to me. The history of revolution and modern evolutionary theory lend credence to Byron's breathtaking assertion. But how frightening! Are cataclysm and catastrophe the birth spasms of the future, is the mass grave some sort of cradle, does the future always arrive borne on a torrent of blood?

In my shul, B'Nai Jeshurun, on the High Holy Days, the rabbis prepare a booklet which contains beautiful and provocative passages from the vast body of Jewish spiritual inquiry and explication. And so this year, 5762, days after the towers fell down, the mushroom cloud still visible in the sky over Manhattan, the acrid smoke from the still-burning fires present in every shift in the wind, I read the following sentence, which suggests another kind of prologue to creation, perhaps offers hope for some prelude other than destruction, some other way for the future to commence; from the Talmud (BT Nedarim 39B):

Repentance preceded the world.

Tony Kushner
New York City
April 11, 2002

TONY KUSHNER's plays include *A Bright Room Called Day*; *Angels in America, Parts One and Two*; *Slavs!*; *Homebody/Kabul*; and *Caroline, or Change*, a musical with composer Jeanine Tesori. He has written adaptations of Corneille's *The Illusion*, S. Ansky's *The Dybbuk* and Brecht's *The Good Person of Szechuan*; as well as English-language libretti for the operas *Brundibar* by Hans Krasa and *Comedy on the Bridge* by Bohuslav Martinu. He wrote the screenplay for the Mike Nichols film of *Angels in America*. Recent books include *Brundibar*, with illustrations by Maurice Sendak; the text for *The Art of Maurice Sendak, 1980–the Present*; and *Wrestling with Zion: Progressive Jewish-American Responses to the Israeli-Palestinian Conflict*, co-edited with Alisa Solomon. Mr. Kushner is the recipient of numerous awards, including the Pulitzer Prize for Drama, two Tony Awards for Best Play, three Obie Awards for Playwriting, the Evening Standard Award, a Whiting Writer's Fellowship, an Arts Award from the American Academy of Arts and Letters, the PEN/Laura Pels Award for a Mid-Career Playwright, a Spirit of Justice Award from the Gay and Lesbian Advocates and Defenders, a Cultural Achievement Award from the National Foundation for Jewish Culture, and an Emmy Award.